Taking Back Your Life...

One Thought at a Time

HARVEST HOUSE PUBLISHERS
EUGENE, OREGON

Cover design by Koechel Peterson and Associates, Minneapolis, Minnesota

TAKING BACK YOUR LIFE...ONE THOUGHT AT A TIME
Formerly published as *Overcoming Negative Emotions*
Copyright © 2014 by Annie Chapman
Published by Harvest House Publishers
Eugene, Oregon 97402
www.harvesthousepublishers.com

Library of Congress Cataloging-in-Publication Data
Chapman, Annie.
[Overcoming negative emotions]
Taking back your life...one thought at a time / Annie Chapman.
    pages cm
Rev. ed. of: Overcoming negative emotions. c2011.
Includes bibliographical references.
ISBN 978-0-7369-5688-8 (pbk.)
ISBN 978-0-7369-5689-5 (eBook)
1. Christian women—Religious life. 2. Emotions—Religious aspects—Christianity. I. Title.
BV4527.C46 2014
248.8'43—dc23
                                                          2013043544

*When I married Steve 35 years ago, I knew he was a good man.
However, I had no idea I was marrying an incredibly talented
author, skilled editor, patient cheerleader, and by far
the nicest person I've ever had the privilege of meeting.*

*If it weren't for his constant encouragement
and incalculable assistance,
I would not have finished this book.*

*Thank you, Steve!
I owe you a huge debt of gratitude—
and I look forward to you collecting on it…
for the next 35 years.*

Acknowledgments

There are many who have helped me find my way through this maze of life. Some of those folks are mentioned in the pages of this book. Because of their invaluable contributions, I have experienced the joy of finding God's truths. I am grateful.

My family has made my life so much fun and fulfilling—Steve, especially! Not only is he a terrific husband and friend, but he is also one incredible pre-editor and sounding board. He keeps me from embarrassing myself. I am humbled.

Eternal gratitude belongs to God the Father, the Son, and the Holy Spirit for the priceless gifts of salvation and restoration. Because I am forgiven, now I can forgive. And because of God's continued work—I am at peace.

Contents

Turn 4: Cleanse your hands

Turn 5: Purify your heart

Foreword

Steve Chapman

As Annie's husband and traveling companion to many of the women's conferences where she speaks, I've heard her often start her time with the ladies with this story:

> A few years ago Steve asked me if there was anything special I wanted as a gift for my birthday. Since I was born in October, and our country was in the middle of an exciting political season at that time, I knew exactly what I wanted. For 30 years Steve and I functioned quite well with only major network television to watch. However, that year I wanted to view the political coverage of the presidential debates on a more fair and balanced cable channel.
>
> Steve caved in to my wishes, and for four glorious years we nearly wore our thumbs out on the remote as we channel-surfed through the vast choices. Though the options were, for the most part, not all that life-changing, I did make a "discovery" of a channel that I enjoyed returning to as often as I could. Its programming highlighted many health and science shows I found interesting and engaging. On one particular day, I watched a documentary of the fertilization of the human egg that I want to tell you about today. When I saw it, I immediately thought of

sharing it with the ladies I'm privileged to speak to, so I'm going to tell you about it.

On this particular episode they showed a yet-to-be-fertilized egg suspended in low light, like a planet hanging in space. Suddenly the scene shifted to a long, dark corridor where there were millions of little "squigglies" making their way toward their destination, which was the egg. I don't even want to think about where they had positioned the little movie camera to capture such fascinating footage. The sperm seemed to be in a race, the kind that would rival the swift and intense runners in a world-class 100-meter run. And it was just as exciting to watch.

As I scooted to the edge of my seat to observe the contest, I noticed that some of the little guys looked a bit sluggish. They meandered along as though they didn't quite have a grasp on what they were supposed to be doing. Others were going in circles, and some even crashed and burned along the way. However, there were a few contenders that would have put Olympic sprinters to shame. These survivors were on an unstoppable quest.

Totally enthralled with the whole process, I found myself cheering as one of them reached the egg. What took place next was a complete shock. I had assumed that it was "winner take all" in the race to the finish line; however, when the first arrival tried to penetrate the egg, it was rebuffed. I didn't realize at the time that there was a hard membrane encasing the egg. Again and again the sperm bounced off. And then I saw it. One little go-getter started boring his head into the egg. Relentlessly he kept at it. Then all of a sudden the shell seemed to crack open and in an instant the "winner" was swallowed into the egg.

What a marvelous sight! Do you know what happened in that unforgettable moment? Life! Pregnancy and a new beginning. Nothing would ever be the same as a result of the meeting of that sperm and egg.

As I prepared my heart for speaking to you today, I once again thought of that documentary. In my mind's eye I saw you as a bunch of eggs expectantly longing for an infusion of life. I don't know if the human egg has a choice as to whether it is fertilized or not, but I do know the human heart has one.

In the time we'll have together here, there will be stories, Scripture passages, poems, and commentary. Whether you allow the hard shell that encapsulates your heart to be penetrated by any of these things will be totally up to you. My greatest hope is the outcome of your time today will be that something I say—maybe a verse of Scripture, a song lyric, or perhaps a story—will find its way into your heart. I can only hope that at the end of our gathering, when you return to your homes, you can say to your loved ones, "I went to a ladies' conference today, and I think I'm pregnant!"

Because I have observed so many ladies respond with excitement to the biblically sound and relatable material Annie offers at her speaking engagements, I'm confident the same will happen when you read this book. This adaptation of one of her most important seminars does in deed have the potential to implant new hope in your heart. In fact, I expect that will happen even before you finish reading this book.

Steve Chapman

Submit therefore to God.
Resist the devil and he will flee from you.
Draw near to God and He will draw near to you.
Cleanse your hands, you sinners;
and purify your hearts, you double-minded.

JAMES 4:7-8

Looking at Life Through "Context" Lenses

O ne of the most common challenges that affect people in my age group (over 50…and that's all I'll say about that) is our weakening eyesight. The world becomes a frustrating blur, and since not all of us are good candidates for corrective laser surgery, the only solution for some of us are the annoying glasses that sit on our noses. While it's true that fading vision in our seasoned years can sometimes cause everything around us to be in a haze, I have happily discovered that there is another type of vision that can get *stronger* by the year. That is, as I get older I can see certain things more clearly than ever. I call this growing advantage the ability to "look at life through *context* lenses."

Gratefully, I've lived long enough that I can look back on my life from the vantage point of maturity, experience, and even some wisdom. Many of the happenings that seemed at the time so horrible and life-defeating are now viewed as events and episodes that taught me more about God's sovereignty and mercy…and in some cases are still teaching me today. Some individuals, for example, who sparked my anger and bitter disappointment years ago are now seen more as instructors in the classroom of life than as the enemies I thought they were. And many decisions I made, both wise and foolish, are no longer sources of arrogant pride or shameful sting. Instead they are interpreted as matters of fact that caused me to know more of God's grace.

With the advantages of time and space between me and the various pains as well as pleasures I've known, it is as though day-by-day I'm getting closer to the valued 20/20 level of clarity regarding life. How have I changed my attitude toward what was once perceived as tragic so that it's now a triumph? Each day I more accurately see how God can ultimately work all things together for good (Romans 8:28). The jagged quilt squares of my life have been made into a meaningful mosaic that is beautiful to see and keeps me warm in these post-midlife years. Only a loving God could work such a miracle.

Along with of a clearer view of the past that my maturity has yielded, another benefit I've experience is that my vision of what I'm supposed to be doing with my life has come into better focus. I am confident that I now can follow the biblical mandate clearly stated in Titus 2:4-5, that the older women are to teach younger women how to live productive lives. Whether it is helping my daughter, Heidi, as she is in the throes of raising small children, teaching a roomful of women at a conference, or encouraging a sister in the hall of a church after a Sunday morning service, my "older woman" status isn't something to be wasted.

I am utterly thankful to Harvest House Publishers for opening the door for me to share my vision with you. Perhaps you've been wondering what to do with your life or you haven't been able to clearly see the path that leads to a full and productive life in the Lord. I pray this book will help you.

The incredibly huge dilemma I face in reaching out to you is that I'm limited to literally a handful of pages. I can only offer some of the many precious truths that have been so meaningful and helpful to me through the years. Though the choice process wasn't easy, I've decided to focus on a portion of the New Testament that has been one of the most pivotal passages for me regarding encouragement, truth, and vision. I believe it will most likely be the same for you too.

I've chosen this passage for two important reasons. First, as a result of personally striving to hear and do what the verses teach, I can report that even though I haven't arrived at the destination of perfection, I have reached the place of emotional healing I so desperately needed.

I now look with greater joy and understanding on my past, my present, and my future.

While it is an exciting privilege to share through this book the personal benefits I've gleaned from this life-changing passage, there is something that brings me even greater delight. My second reason for choosing this portion of Scripture is my hope that after hearing and benefiting from the wisdom found in God's Word you too, in time, will experience the wonderful advantage of seeing life through "context" lenses. The thought of what lies ahead for you thrills me. And I'm so glad we're going to have some time together to learn and grow.

Trusting God's GPS

An old Indian was teaching his grandson about life and said to the boy, "A fight is going on inside me. It is a terrible fight, and it is between two wolves. One is evil—he is anger, envy, sorrow, regret, greed, arrogance, self-pity, guilt, resentment, inferiority, lies, false pride, superiority, and ego. The other is good—he is joy, peace, love, hope, serenity, humility, kindness, benevolence, empathy, generosity, truth, compassion, and faith."

The grandfather sighed and continued, "This same fight is going on inside you—and inside every other person too."

The grandson thought about it for a minute and then asked his grandfather, "Which wolf will win?"

Replied the grandfather, "The one you feed."[1]

Along with much of America, I watched the report on the news about a young couple who was driving 180 miles to see family for the Christmas holidays. They left on Christmas Eve with their young baby in the backseat with plenty of time to arrive for the family festivities. One of the early gifts the couple had given to one another was a Global Positioning System unit for their car. They were excited to have a chance to play with their new toy. Upon departing their home they typed in their destination and waited for the machine to tell them the best way to travel.

The GPS mapped out the suggested route for them to follow. However, instead of taking them safely to their family, they ended up on an unpaved logging road that was buried in several feet of snow. They used their new video camera to document what they feared would be the last few hours of their lives. The footage was heartbreaking to say the least. Fortunately, their worst fears were not realized. Unlike many other "lost" tales, this young couple's misadventure had a happy ending. After many scary hours of cold and hunger, they were rescued. Although they were a day late and physically suffering from the effects of the frigid weather, they arrived safe and sound at their destination.

I too have been lost. I have been down a dark, cold road spiritually and emotionally. My senses of well-being and trust were nearly destroyed. It began early in my life. As I revealed in my book *Letting Go of Anger,* my childhood was marred and violated by the assault of a lustful stranger.[2] The sinful act of this man threw me off the path of peace and left me stranded in a place of frozen bitterness and stabbing anger. I feared it was a desolate place I would be stuck in forever.

However, with unreserved gratitude to God who works all things to the good of His own, my story that began in tragedy doesn't continue that way. Though I encountered such a frightening detour in those early years, I am now acquainted with the "peace of God, which surpasses all understanding" (Philippians 4:7 NKJV). When I needed it most, I was introduced to what could be called "God's GPS"—His written Word, the Bible. This trustworthy guidance system led me to peace many years ago, and it still helps me avoid the dead ends on life's roads today. I fully agree with Martin Luther who said, "The Bible is alive, it speaks to me; it has feet, it runs after me; it has hands, it lays hold of me. The Bible is not antique or modern. It is eternal."

Somewhat like the modern GPS that has a seemingly endless amount of the earth's highway information loaded into it, the Bible is filled with even more helpful guidance about the lay of the spiritual and emotional territories where we live—and it will never steer us wrong. Because of the immensity of the content of the Word, and because every line in the Bible is extremely important to all who journey with

God, it is very difficult to choose just one passage to offer as "the most helpful." But as I mentioned in the introduction, there are two verses of Scripture I will highlight in these pages. Why not write them down, read them often or memorize them, and quote them as much as possible as an encouragement as you travel through this book?

> *Submit therefore to God.*
> *Resist the devil and he will flee from you.*
> *Draw near to God and He will draw near to you.*
> *Cleanse your hands, you sinners;*
> *and purify your hearts, you double-minded.*
>
> JAMES 4:7-8

The reason these few lines out of all the Bible have been so meaningful to me is that they include five turns that I (and many others) have made on the road of life that have led me back to spiritual safety. And they continue to keep me safe.

Each line of the passage is connected to the next, so if the first one isn't completed, you likely won't get to the second, and without following the first two, you may not get to the third, and so on. In essence, God, in His unmatched ability to order things, has arranged the directions so that one step will lead you to the next...and so on until you reach the destination of wholeness and holiness.

· · · · ·

The goal of this book is to help you reach the
destination of a heart filled with peace and joy.

· · · · ·

Perhaps you lost your way when you placed your trust in a person who, though he or she promised to be faithful to you, abandoned you to the feelings of loneliness or loss. Maybe you followed an errant doctrine that has left you wandering around spiritually confused. Or could it be that you set your sights on money and success, only to find both of them bankrupt and unfulfilling?

Whatever or whomever it was that may have guided you or encouraged you down a daunting or discouraging road, please consider making the turns the James passage offers. In the pages that follow, we're going to look closely at each of them. Through examples and stories from my life and others as it relates to the specific directive, I hope you'll be inspired and encouraged to make any changes needed. Although I won't always stay with the GPS/map theme, the goal of this book is to help you reach the destination of a heart filled with peace and joy.

Since these directions from James are in the Bible, which is readily available to most people, it's tragic when someone fails to take them to heart and misses out on what God has planned for him or her. I know my life would be bereft if I'd never discovered and implemented these words of wisdom. Too many of us have "God's GPS"—the Bible—but we never use it. Some of us hear excellent directions from the Word, but never do the necessary work of following them. To arrive at wholeness and holiness, hearing these truths from James must be supported by doing the steps. If you do want to reach that destination, don't you think it's time to start heading in that direction?

Here we go!

Turn 1

"Submit to God."

2

Responding to God

The first step out of any spiritual or emotional wilderness begins with submitting our lives to God. The word "submit" is a military term that means "like a private in the army obeys the general." Just as the decision to "sign up" for military service changes the life of a person, when we submit to God it changes everything about our lives.

My husband, Steve, and I live just a few miles from Fort Campbell, Kentucky, the home of the 101st Airborne Division (Air Assault), the 5th Special Forces Group (Airborne), the 160th Special Operations Aviation Regiment (Airborne), the 86th Combat Support Hospital, the 716th MP Battalion, and the training ground for numerous Army National Guard and Army Reserve units. When I shop in nearby Clarksville, Tennessee, which is the neighboring town to the base, I see armed service personnel everywhere. It's not difficult to identify those who have enlisted in the military. I can tell by the clothes they wear, the cut of their hair, and the places they live. Even the way they carry themselves is a giveaway that they are part of the armed forces. I'm sure that submitting to the authority of the United States military was not a casual decision these soldiers made.

And the same is true when we submit our lives to our heavenly General. Nothing is the same afterward.

Are You Sure You've Chosen Jesus?

Unfortunately, not everyone who thinks they are submitted to God really is. This is revealed in some unsettling verses in Matthew 7, where Jesus says, "Not everyone who says to Me, 'Lord, Lord' will enter the kingdom of heaven, but he who does the will of My Father who is in heaven will enter. Many will say to Me on that day, 'Lord, Lord, did we not prophesy in Your name, and in Your name cast out demons, and in Your name perform many miracles?' And then I will declare to them, 'I never knew you; depart from Me, you who practice lawlessness'" (verses 21-23).

A few years ago I met a woman who discovered she was one of the souls who was in the category of "not everyone who says 'Lord, Lord' will enter the kingdom." An especially unique detail of her story was that she was a faithful and devoted pastor's wife. Steve and I conducted a Sunday morning service for the congregation her husband pastors. (Steve and I are Christian musicians who give concerts and are frequently invited to lead special church services.) Following the service, the four of us went out for lunch. We made our selections from the menu and waited for the food to arrive. After a few minutes of verbal niceties, this woman turned to me and said, "I would like to give you my personal testimony." I said I would love to hear it. She proceeded to tell me her story. (And with her permission I'm sharing it with you.)

Charlene began by telling me that she'd filled the role as pastor's wife for more than 30 years, but she had only been a Christian for the past 18 months. With that statement she had my full attention. She assured me that she had been an excellent and supportive wife all those years. She said, "I read my Bible every day, prayed, played the piano for church services, taught Sunday school, and faithfully attended church each Sunday."

She shared that when she was a little girl of six, she, along with her Sunday school class, walked forward to receive Christ. However, throughout her growing-up years she experienced nagging doubts that caused her to wonder if she truly was a Christian. Every time she expressed her uncertainty concerning her salvation, her parents responded, "Of course you're a Christian, Charlene. Don't you remember when you were a little girl and you and your class went forward to receive Jesus? The devil is trying to make you doubt your salvation." Charlene said she accepted her parents' explanation on the surface, but always in the back of her mind was the thought that perhaps she was not a true believer.

Time went on, and in her early twenties she met, fell in love with, and married a young man who was studying to become a pastor. From time to time doubt about her spiritual condition would return, and she would candidly say to him, "I'm not sure I'm a Christian." His reply was not unlike her parents': "Of course you're saved! The devil is just messing with your mind."

Her husband eventually graduated and was hired as a pastor. They were both active in their church. The Lord blessed them with two children. In the course of their lives, events took place that threatened their children's emotional and physical health. As Charlene went before the Lord to pray for them, she often sensed deep in her heart that she wasn't connecting with God. One day she thought with frightening force, *I don't really know God, and He doesn't know me.*

Tears formed in my new friend's eyes as she told me about sitting alone in the quiet of her living room and praying to receive Christ. With that conscious and deliberate act of her will, she finally settled the matter. From that moment on, she testified, "All the doubts that had plagued me were no longer there. For the first time in my life I knew absolutely that I had truly *submitted* my all to Christ."

Excited about what had happened, the first thing Charlene wanted to do was tell her husband! She got into her car and went straight to the church. She found him in his office. She walked in and stood before him at his desk. He looked up, surprised to see her.

"I have something very important to tell you," she shared.

He lovingly said, "I'm busy right now. Can it wait until later?"

"Yes, it can. Let me know when you have time to talk," she said.

Later that week her husband came to her and asked, "What did you want to tell me the other day that you were so excited about?"

After she told him that she had prayed to receive Christ and that now she was sure she was a Christian for the first time in her life, he apologized for delaying her joy in sharing such momentous news. He was thrilled for her. She said, "I feel I should walk down the aisle at church and make a public profession of my faith. And I think I should to do it at the end of the second service next Sunday."

Her husband asked her if he could share with the first service what she planned to do. She agreed and spent the remainder of the week preparing her testimony. She could hardly wait to make her decision to fully submit to Christ public.

As she arrived at church for the second service, she was met by her husband. He was filled with joy as he told her that earlier that morning dozens of people had come forward to receive Christ as a result of his sharing her testimony with them. Among the many who had publicly proclaimed their allegiance to Jesus during the first service were a few deacons, some elders, and a couple of Sunday school teachers. Many of them had suffered the same doubts through the years that Charlene had.

After hearing Charlene's testimony at the second service, many others, including some the pastor had assumed were believers, came to the altar to submit to Christ. By the time the day's services had ended, more than 100 people had prayed and received Christ as their Savior! My friend laughingly told me that the report that spread through the community was that "revival broke out the Sunday the pastor's wife got saved."

For a long time I pondered that conversation I had with Charlene. One of the most touching details of her story was how she finally responded to her deep longing to have a real relationship with Christ. She cried out to Him in a prayer of repentance and submission. And God heard and responded.

Crying Out to God

How important is that cry of sorrow and desire? Have you ever been in a delivery room when a baby was being born? I have been there on three occasions—twice when my children were delivered and once when I was serving as a Lamaze coach for an expectant woman whose husband couldn't be with her. When the labor was done and that sweet little bundle of humanity had squeezed his way down the dark corridor of flesh, the room remained ominously quiet until something very important happened. There were no cheers of victory, no squeals of delight until we heard the baby cry. The louder the cry, the greater the celebration. The cry was the sign of life.

• • • • •

You don't have to pray a certain prayer; you simply
need to invite Christ to come in and take up
residence in your heart, soul, mind, and spirit.

• • • • •

My new friend Charlene had shared that she was doing all the right things as a sweet pastor's wife. She was living the right kind of life and being the best wife and mother she knew how to be. However, there was something missing. There was no cry in her, and she knew it. No matter what anyone else said to convince her that she was all right, she knew the truth.

Perhaps you see yourself in this story. Maybe you have lived with nagging doubt, wondering if you have submitted your to life to Jesus. You may realize there is no "cry" in you. I encourage you right now to stop reading these pages, bow your head, and take care of any doubts once and for all. You don't have to pray a certain prayer; you simply need to invite Christ to come in and take up residence in your heart, soul, mind, and spirit. Then you need to submit to His service and come under His authority. You can become a private in God's army. Today would be a great day to sign up for duty.

If you have yet to submit your life to Christ, perhaps these steps and verses from God's Word will encourage you to make that choice of faith.

- Admit your sin and your need for God's forgiveness. Romans 3:23 says, "For all have sinned and fall short of the glory of God." Forgiveness is a universal need.

- Acknowledge that God has provided a way to be free from sin. Romans 5:8 says, "God demonstrates His own love toward us, in that while we were yet sinners, Christ died for us." This is a universal gift.

- Admit that Jesus satisfied the penalty for your sin. John 3:16 says, "God so loved the world, that He gave His only begotten Son, that whoever believes in Him shall not perish, but have eternal life." This is a universal invitation.

- Invite Christ to take up residence in your life. Romans 10:9-10 says, "If you confess with your mouth Jesus as Lord, and believe in your heart that God raised Him from the dead, you will be saved; for with the heart a person believes, resulting in righteousness, and with the mouth he confesses, resulting in salvation." This is a universal promise.

If you just "cried out" with a prayer of submission to God, or you've done it in the past, congratulations! You have taken the first and correct turn to finding your way out of life's wilderness. Share this exciting news with someone you're close to who will encourage you in your new life of faith.

Working Together

Before we look at the next turn God has mapped out in our James 4 verses, I encourage you to understand that submitting to and following God is not one-sided. Walking with God is not a performance, as if you are an *American Idol* contestant and He is the celestial judge who might say "Great job!" or "You're not good enough." Nor is it a solo on God's part, where we step back and let Him do everything. Instead, our relationship with God is, in essence, a "divine duet."

3

Walking in Harmony with God

*God provides food for the birds, but
He doesn't drop it into their nest.*

AUTHOR UNKNOWN

Submit therefore to God" (James 4:7). Submitting to God doesn't mean we sit down and do nothing. For far too many years I didn't understand this truth and viewed my relationship with my Father in heaven as a passive one. Like so many other children of my generation, I sang with great gusto and wholehearted assurance the familiar lyrics of "Jesus Loves Me": "Little ones to Him belong; they are weak, but He is strong."

Although there have never been truer words written, I had concluded that since God is strong and I am weak, I was incapable of doing anything for myself. This led me to believe that it was God's responsibility to do everything for me since He is the strong one in our relationship. I thought my only job in our Father/child union was to pray and make my requests known to Him. God's job was to answer my requests with either a "yes," "no," or "not now" response.

Having this attitude of uninvolved dependence on God was not only unbiblical, but it was actually a formula for failure. In my case it turned out to be a lazy cop-out. This errant thinking was very evident when it came to one of my lifelong struggles. As long as I can remember I've battled excess weight. Regretfully, I've spent many precious years engaging in a major war for control over my appetite. Like many people, I was often overtaken by the intensity of the struggle. Too many times I waved the white flag of surrender as I conceded that victory was too difficult and not worth the price required. So I chose to do nothing. I refused to engage in the battle anymore. However, the lack of self-control over my eating habits and discontent about my appearance were always sources of shame and self-condemnation.

My lopsided belief that God was responsible for doing everything didn't help me when it came to my battle with bulge. Since I was totally weak, I considered my participation in weight loss to be solely one of prayer. And pray I did. Each night before I went to sleep I would sincerely ask the Lord, "Please, Father, make me lose weight. I put my trust in You and believe with my whole heart that when I wake up in the morning, I will be thin. And, Lord, when I'm at the grocery store, please make me not buy the potato chips. And if I am weak and buy them, please don't let me eat them. And if I happen to eat them, would You please remove all the fat and empty calories from them? God, help me and make me skinny."

While I naively thought praying was my only responsibility, I did recognize that God's part in my weight loss endeavor was the more challenging. He was supposed to supernaturally cause fat cells to disappear or at least permanently deflate them—preferably while I slept. He was supposed to miraculously turn empty caloric foods into nutritious manna and transform junk food into organic fruits and vegetables. Or, as I heard a comedienne once say, "Please turn these french fries into carrot sticks."

As strange as it may seem, it never occurred to me that I was supposed to participate in the answer to my prayers. I was a lot like the person who said, "I would do anything to lose weight. Well, anything except eat right and exercise. Other than that, I would do anything."

A one-sided relationship with God comes in very handy when things don't turn out like I prayed. When I piously claim I have no strength of my own and that the outcome is all up to God, then it's easier to blame Him when it doesn't pan out the way I requested. When the pounds were still there the morning after my earnest prayer for fat removal, what was I to conclude? Either God was not powerful enough to answer my prayer or He didn't love me and wanted me to be fat. Either way, it wasn't my fault.

The consequences of this type of thinking can be severe. I heard about an unwed teenage couple several years ago who was flirting with a sexual relationship. As they rode in a car on their way to a "no tell motel" in the next city, they held hands and prayed, "God, if you don't want us to have sex tonight, please make us have a flat tire on the way to the motel." Unfortunately they arrived at the "Sleaze Inn" with all four tires fully inflated and an empty cup of self control.

* * * * *

God takes the lead in life's song, but unless we
are willing to sing harmony with Him, we will
miss out on a beautiful, melodious symphony.

* * * * *

This young couple is a perfect example that there are times when ignorance is not bliss, it's just plain dumb and dangerous. There were buckets of hot, angry tears and accusing barbs aimed at God when they ended up, at 19 years of age, pregnant out of wedlock. They couldn't believe God hadn't answered their prayer and tearfully moaned, "How could God let this happen to us? We prayed and asked Him to stop us. He let us down."

Oh the pain that could have been avoided if they had understood that they were not to be bystanders in their relationship with God but active participants. Our heavenly Father is not doing a solo performance for our benefit. Instead, we are to be engaged in a harmonious duet with Him. The paradoxical truth is we *are* helpless without God's power. Nonetheless, we must do our part in this lyrical relationship. God takes the lead in life's song, but unless we are willing to sing harmony with Him, we will miss out on a beautiful, melodious symphony.

God's Part/Our Part

I have no problem acknowledging my total dependence on the Lord. I know without a doubt that the wise thing to do each morning when I awake is to say, "God, I need Your gift of strength to live for You today. Without it I am hopeless!" That's a prayer that comes readily from my heart. The greater revelation and challenge for me was to realize that I could and was expected to *contribute* to the quality of my daily spiritual life. Two instances in my life stand out in revealing that submitting to God and working *with* Him are great opportunities that I shouldn't overlook.

The first one comes from something I learned from our son when he was in the eighth grade. What I gleaned from Nathan not only altered my way of thinking, but it changed my life. Here's how our junior high kid taught me a college-level lesson.

Up until his middle-school years I homeschooled Nathan. Although it can be quite a challenge to home-educate a child, especially in his or her middle school grades, for the most part our experience was going fairly smoothly. Until seventh grade. That year proved particularly difficult for teacher and student. It was filled with the usual distractions that come with schooling at home, but we had an additional unexpected biological challenge. Within a 12-month span, Nathan grew 12 inches and gained 60 pounds. The trauma of such rapid physical growth overshadowed anything we were trying to do in his home studies. There is a significant degree of physical pain associated with growing so quickly. Nathan's back hurt, his legs ached, and his knees were adversely affected. With most of his energy focused on growing, there was little left for studying subjects that he, for the most part, found boring and irrelevant to his daily life. Nathan and I were both happy when that school year ended, and we were both extremely relieved we were still alive and speaking to each other.

When it was time to consider what we were going to do for Nathan's eighth grade year, memories of the previous year flashed before my bloodshot eyes. I told Steve, "We have to put Nathan in regular school and let someone else enjoy him for a while…or Nathan and I might end up maiming each other." We decided to send him to a local Christian school for the eighth grade.

One morning, well into the school year, we were sitting at the breakfast table together. Nathan announced that he was scheduled to have a very important exam that day. He then added a little detail: He had failed to study for it. "But," Nathan assured us, "don't worry, I've prayed about it." For some strange reason telling us that he'd "prayed about it" did little to quiet my concern over his academic future.

A few days later Nathan got his test score back: 50%. His reaction to his poor performance was what opened my eyes to a tremendous spiritual truth. He said, "See! God did His part. If I'd done mine, I would have gotten 100 percent right."

This simple but profound admission was pivotal in my spiritual understanding. I realized that yes, I must pray and submit my ways to the Lord, but I must also be willing to do my part.

The second eye-opening moment for me regarding the divine duet reality centers around a health incident. This one is more personal and involves my heart and that dreaded sticky stuff called cholesterol.

There is a lot of heart disease in my family. My grandfather died of a heart attack in his early sixties. My mother battled heart disease until cancer took her in 1996. My father had a massive heart attack at age 51 and nearly died. He had to deal with the residuals of this condition until he passed on in 1998. You might think that knowing about this weakness in my family's medical history would make me more careful about taking care of my ticker. Sadly, that has not always been the case. Finally feeling rather convicted over my lack of attention to my health, I decided to get my cholesterol checked. As I feared, it was well above recommended levels.

At that point, to say I was concerned about my heart health would have been an understatement. In fact, I laid hands on myself and prayed, "Oh, God! My cholesterol is far beyond what it should be. You are the Great Physician. I know You are able to fix what is broken. Please make my cholesterol come down. Touch my body and heal me." As I was praying, my mind suddenly returned to the words of Nathan long ago when he was an eighth grader: "God did His part. If I had done mine, I would have made 100 percent."

Oh, yes, the divine duet. I continued to pray about my health, but my prayer took a slightly different turn: "I know You can heal me. I know You will do Your part. I commit to doing my part. Instead of bacon and eggs, I'll start eating oatmeal. Instead of sitting on the couch watching television, I'll start walking every day. I'll limit the time I spend listening to talk radio because it contributes to my soaring blood pressure. To reduce my stress level, I'll fill our house with peaceful sounds of praise and worship. I'll make room in my heart for more of Your Word."

My doctor had informed me that some of the many factors that contributed to my elevated cholesterol were my family history, poor food choices, a sedentary lifestyle that lacked physical exercise, and a stress-filled environment. Of these four factors, I had the potential to control or directly affect three of them. I couldn't do anything about my ancestors, but perhaps I could make a positive impact on my descendants.

For six months I faithfully did my part while holding tightly to the assurance that God was doing His part. When I went back to the doctor and had my cholesterol numbers checked again, I was thrilled to hear they had dropped 66 points. It was a good outcome that was accomplished without medication. I did my part, and God did his.

Keeping the Focus

Understanding the need to do our part to successfully live by the divine duet principle in no way diminishes the incredible importance of maintaining an attitude of total dependence on God. To make sure I don't fall into this error, I remind myself that without God's help there is no way I can do my part. And almost every morning I note this undeniable truth when I dry my hair. The blow dryer I use is a small appliance that lies cold, silent, and useless on the counter until I pick it up, plug it in, and turn it on. Then, and only then, can it fulfill its designed function. In the same way, I know I'm helpless, weak, and useless without the powerful source of the Holy Spirit active in my life. Without God's power given to us to participate in the divine duet, we can't accomplish what we are designed to do.

Our Partnership with God

Throughout the Scriptures we can see the partnership between God and people and the benefits we get.

Revelation 3:20: "Behold, I stand at the door and knock; if anyone hears My voice and opens the door, I will come in to him and will dine with him, and he with Me."

God's part: Stand at our door and knock.

Our part: When the knock is heard, open the door.

End result: An intimate relationship with Him.

Romans 8:28: "We know [we're absolutely certain] that God causes all things to work together for good to those who love God, to those who are called according to His purpose."

Our part: Love God.

God's part: Take the tragic, unforeseen events that leave us shattered and supernaturally make the pieces work together for our ultimate good.

End result: We participate in the greatest of all successes—God's purposes!

Deuteronomy 1:8: "I have placed the land before you; go in and possess the land which the LORD swore to give to your fathers, to Abraham, to Isaac, and to Jacob, to them and their descendants after them."

Look at the divine duet for the children of Israel. It was an 11-day journey from Mt. Sinai to the Promised Land. God gave the land that was flowing with milk and honey into the hands of the Israelites. There was, however, one stipulation before the children of Israel could take up residence: They had to *take* the land. God's part was to give them the land; their part was to take it.

God's people were to enter the Promised Land by way of the wilderness. They were to face the giants God had promised were already defeated foes. They were to march in and take custody of what had already been battled for and won. But because the children of Israel wouldn't do their part, they wandered in the wilderness for 40 years. Immobilized by fear of the enemy and lacking trust that God would deliver them, many of them died without ever experiencing God's promised gift. Tragically, they died in the wilderness rather than face the already-defeated giants. They lost everything because they were too fearful to take the land that God had given them. Scripture reports God's response to their hesitance: "Yet you were not willing to go up, but rebelled against the command of the LORD your God" (Deuteronomy 1:26).

I beg you to not make the mistake the Israelites made. Instead, take hold of the power source—God—and start doing your part. It might be, so to speak, an 11-day journey for you to the milk and honey of victory and joy, but that's a lot shorter than 40 years! There's no need for wandering around in the wilderness of your agony when you know what to do to "take the land" God wants you to enjoy.

God's part: Promise to give us the land and will help us take it.

Our part: See the land, go in, and possess it.

End result: We get to live in a place of peace and provision.

Jeremiah 29:11: "'For I know the plans that I have for you,' declares the LORD, 'plans for welfare and not for calamity to give you a future and a hope. Then you will call upon Me and come and pray to Me, and I will listen to you. You will seek Me and find Me when you search for Me with all your heart. I will be found by you,' declares the LORD."

How sweet of God to play seek-and-find with us. He never hides from us. Just like a lot of parents, I have played hide-and-seek with my children. The game is always played with the goal of being found. If I did too good of a job hiding and the children were getting frustrated or upset about not finding me, I would "accidentally" giggle or knock something over. I would do something so they would know I was nearby. God does the same thing. He is *always* close, wanting to be found. He essentially promised, "If you seek Me, you will find Me. If you knock, I will open the door. If you ask, you will receive because I will give." That is the divine duet at its basic best and is beautifully illustrated in 1 Chronicles 28:9: "For the LORD searches all hearts, and understands every intent of the thoughts. If you seek Him, He will let you find Him; but if you forsake Him, He will reject you forever."

Our part: Call upon the Lord and seek Him.
God's part: To let us find Him.
End result: Hope.

Psalm 14:2: "The LORD has looked down from heaven upon the sons of men to see if there are any who understand, who seek after God."

I once heard this passage interpreted as "God is patiently looking down, waiting for someone to look up at Him." To put it yet another way, someone said, "God shows favor to those who look His way." Though these are paraphrases, I believe they are right on because of something that happened several years ago.

One year we decided we wanted a dog. To be more accurate, Steve and the children decided they wanted a dog. I entertained the idea just to be nice. Because I suspected, based on experience, that I would be the one who would ultimately end up doing the work of feeding, walking, and potty training the pup, I was less than enthusiastic about the acquisition of a furry little critter. However, the children's pleading melted my mother's heart, and my pity for my husband, who had been deprived of the joys of pet ownership as a child, swayed me to the other side. I gave in.

Steve and the children took it upon themselves to scout out the newspapers for advertisements offering puppies for sale. They eventually made contact with a lady to see the pups she had available.

One memorable Saturday morning Steve and the kiddos made the 200-mile round trip journey to meet the breeder. When they arrived they were greeted by five precious puppies safely locked in a large cage. As the roly-poly canines auditioned for their perspective masters, they were at their adorable best. Some of them playfully nipped at each other's ears, while others cutely headed for the back of the cage for the security of distance from the humanoids. However, there was one little black-and-white darling who locked eyes with Steve. Slowly and deliberately the pup walked from the back of the cage to the front of it, never losing Steve's gaze.

Steve said, "When he looked at me I knew he was the one. He looked at me, and I chose him."

As simplistic as this sounds, this is a beautiful picture of our pursuit of our Holy God. When anyone says they "found the Lord" my mind goes back to that Saturday morning when Steve chose Bob. Steve and the kids took the initiative to call the woman. They drove the distance and found her house. They selected Bob to be our very own. I think of Bob's totally helpless state. He was in no position to find us. He was locked away in a cage, unable to free himself from his situation. If he could have gotten free of his puppy prison, there is no way he could have ever found us. Even if he knew where we lived, the distance between where he was and our home was too great for him to cover. Bob might have thought by looking at Steve and showing a willingness to come home with him that he was the one making the choice to be part of our family. However we all know that it was Steve who chose Bob.

God's part: Look down from heaven.

Our part: Seek (look up for) God.

End result: We get to be part of God's family!

> The Lord still waits for you to come to him so he can show you his love...for the Lord is faithful to his promises (Isaiah 30:18 MSG).

Joshua 1:9: "Have I not commanded you? Be strong and courageous! Do not tremble or be dismayed, for the LORD your God is with you wherever you go."

God's part: Stay with us wherever we go.

Our part: Choose courage; don't tremble.

End result: Living in the comfort of His awesome presence.

Psalm 27:13: "I would have despaired unless I had believed that I would see the goodness of the LORD in the land of the living. Wait for the LORD; be strong and let your heart take courage; yes, wait for the LORD."

Erroneously I believed for many years that the word "wait" was passive. Sometimes when I heard "You need to wait on the Lord," I'd get a mental image of me impatiently sitting in a waiting room. I'd be twiddling my thumbs, pacing back and forth, killing time while I waited for something to happen.

However, the accurate word picture for "waiting" is one of action. It depicts being twisted together or bonded together, sort of like a pretzel that is so entwined that no one can distinguish where it starts or ends. We are to bind ourselves to God like this.

I've been on the receiving end of the "twisting" together, which helped me better understand why we can derive courage from such an action. One Christmas our granddaughter Lily decided to take advantage of the opportunity to sing a song for her daddy's office Christmas party. The selection she chose was one that is an important part of our Christmas celebration. *O, I Wonder* was the same song Steve's mother had taught him as a little boy. When our daughter, Heidi, was about five years old, we picked up that musical mantle and passed it along to her. In keeping with family tradition, Heidi passed it along to Lily.

I happened to be standing beside Lily as she began her four-year-old rendition of the song. She started with her little arm casually looped around my leg just above my knee. As the song continued and she got more and more nervous her grip around my leg got tighter and tighter. I began to worry that by the time the song was finished all the blood to and from my lower extremity would be halted. However, the tighter she twisted her little body around my leg, the more I encouraged and comforted her by patting her on the back as she sang.

When she finished the tune, the applause was fun for all of us to hear. Though her singing debut was a success, I'll never forget how Lily, in the stress and intimidation of the moment, had reached out and twisted herself to a person she perceived to be bigger and stronger and very loving. In the same way, I've determined to respond to the frightening things that happen in my life by clinging to the One who is bigger, stronger, and who loves me. When I'm afraid, I grab hold of God and won't let go. I wait on the Lord and know that as I do my part, He will gently pat me on my back and give me the courage to face whatever is ahead.

God's part: Provide His goodness, safety, and direction.

Our part: Wait for the Lord.

End result: Absence of despair; infusion of hope in our lives.

Proverbs 28:13: "He who conceals his transgressions will not prosper, but he who confesses and forsakes them will find compassion."

Our part: Confess our sins.

God's part: Be faithful and righteous and forgive us our sins; cleanse us from unrighteousness.

End result: God's compassion and the prosperity of His righteousness poured into our hearts.

Philippians 2:5,7: "Have this attitude in yourselves which was also in Christ Jesus...[who] emptied Himself, taking the form of a bond-servant." (These verses could very well be the most challenging of all divine duet opportunities. However, the outcome is probably the most treasured.)

It is a beautiful thing to see how the God of the universe chooses to limit Himself in order to have relationships with us. When I walk with my young granddaughter Lily, I deliberately make my steps fit her tiny stride. When I'm walking with my grownup friends, they tease me about my overly determined pace. (I inherited my tendency to nearly run when I walk from my mother.) You see, I am not walking with Lily simply to get to a destination or to expend some sweat. No, I'm walking with her because I want to be with her, to spend time with her. *It's all about relationship.* Lily can't keep up if I use my exercise or get-somewhere pace, but I can slow and shorten my stride to match hers.

Also, when we play games together, I intentionally give up my matured skills so the game will last longer, I can spend more time with her, and I can encourage her participation and growth. Everything about our time together is about relationship.

In similar ways, God deliberately limits Himself to have personal relationships with you and me. We can't go to His level, so He comes down to ours.

Our part: Humble ourselves.

God's part: Willingly limits His abilities and encourages relationship with us.

End result: We are blessed, and we become blessings to others by living in the attitude of our loving, ever-serving God.

Our Part/His Part Worksheet

To further solidify the "divine duet" truth in your heart, consider the following passages and fill in the blanks.

John 3:16: "For God so loved the world, that He gave His only begotten Son, that whoever believes in Him shall not perish, but have eternal life."

Our part:

God's part:

End result:

Philippians 4:6-7: "Be anxious for nothing, but in everything by prayer and supplication with thanksgiving let your requests be made known to God. And the peace of God which surpasses all comprehension, will guard your hearts and your minds in Christ Jesus."

Our part:

God's part:

End result:

2 Corinthians 6:17-18: "'Therefore come out from their midst and be separate,' says the Lord...'And I will welcome you. And I will be a father to you, and you shall be sons and daughters to me.'"

Our part:

God's part:

End result:

James 4:8: "Draw near to God and He will draw near to you."

Our part:

God's part:

End result:

Ephesians 6:11: "Put on the full armor of God, so that you will be able to stand firm against the schemes of the devil."

Our part:

God's part:

End result:

1 John 1:9: "If we confess our sins, He is faithful and righteous to forgive us our sins and to cleanse us from all unrighteousness."

Our part:

God's part:

End result:

Matthew 6:14: "If you forgive others for their transgressions, your heavenly Father will also forgive you."

Our part:

God's part:

End result:

Hebrews 12:1-2: "Since we have so great a cloud of witnesses surrounding us, let us also lay aside every encumbrance and the sin which so easily entangles us, and let us run with endurance the race that is set before us, fixing our eyes on Jesus, the author and perfecter of faith."

Our part:

God's part:

End result:

Matthew 6:25,33: "Do not be worried about your life, as to what you will eat or what you will drink; nor for your body, as to what you will put on. Is not life more than food, and the body more than clothing?..."

Seek first [God's] kingdom and His righteousness, and all these things will be added to you."

Our part:

God's part:

End result:

Turn 2

"Resist the devil and he will flee."

4

Silencing the Devil's Whispers

After you have made the first corrective turn by submitting your life to God, the next direction listed is "resist the devil and he will flee from you" (James 4:7).

Our part: Resist the devil.

God's part: Make sure the enemy flees from us.

End result: Success!

Did you notice that the scripture verse doesn't say *if* the devil comes? The implication is definitely *when* the devil approaches, we are to resist him. Furthermore, the Bible tells us our enemy will come at us often and from many directions! Deuteronomy 28:1,7 highlights a promise God made to the Israelites that is as applicable today as it was to His children in ancient times:

> Now it shall be, if you diligently obey the LORD your God, being careful to do all His commandments which I command you today, the LORD your God will set you high above all the nations of the earth…The LORD shall cause your enemies who rise up against you to be defeated before you; they will come out against you one way and will flee before you seven ways.

Our part: Diligently obey the Lord.

God's part: Cause our enemies to be defeated before us.
End result: Our enemies will flee.

I encourage you to memorize these two verses from Deuteronomy and refer to them often to refresh your belief in God's ability and willingness to do His part when you do yours. Isn't it incredible to realize that when we stand firm in resisting the enemy of our souls in this visible world, God works in the unseen world to see to it that the devil takes flight? We can return to the promise that He will do that for us as often as needed. What a blessing!

Now that we know the devil will come to us and is already defeated, the next urgent question to address is, "How will he come to us?" We want to be prepared so we'll recognize even his most subtle attacks. One way he comes is in voices. He whispers in our ears so no one else can hear his temptation offerings. Unfortunately, his whisper is usually loud and clear to us. On rare occasions his voice might be soft and cooing, but for the most part, Satan's voice isn't gentle. Learning to recognize his voice is critical to being ready to resist him.

First Peter 5:8 provides much-needed wisdom to help us prepare for the vocal attacks of the enemies that threaten and entice us to leave God's path of righteousness. Because the devil wants us where it is unsafe, deadly, and dangerous, Peter tells us, "Be of sober spirit, be on the alert. Your adversary, the devil, prowls around like a roaring lion, seeking someone to devour."

Notice that the devil, who is constantly hungry for the souls of men and women, gives advance warning of his presence by roaring. The best way to detect the devil's voice is to study God's Word daily so we know God's voice and can recognize His wisdom. The more we listen to the voice of our Father in heaven, the easier it will be to recognize the deceptions of the father of lies.

In the same way money experts study the details and feel of the "real thing" so they can more readily recognize counterfeit money, we should study God's Word and wisdom so we will know when He is not the one speaking.

In the following chapters, as we go through some of the ways the enemy whispers to you and me, we'll also note the details of his approach and uncover the best responses to counter his proffered temptations. There is an answer to the enemy's voiced threats and temptations that invariably silences him—the Word of God. This is how Jesus responded when Satan tempted Him in the wilderness. Our Lord and Savior repeatedly said, "It is written" and then quoted God's Word to defuse Satan's devilment and stop his destruction.

As you use God's Word, you'll discover that the devil can't defeat the authority of God. And Satan never will be able to. We can rejoice because we have the upper hand in this battle through Jesus Christ. Are you ready to improve your arsenal for resisting the devil? Then let's get started. And as you sense the enemy fleeing, be sure to praise God for helping you do your part and then for doing His part.

5

Understanding What "Forgiven" Means

As we've established, studying what's real helps us recognize coun-terfeits. So looking closely at how forgiving our Lord is will help us recognize when the voice we're hearing is from our enemy and accuser. Consider the numerous biblical accounts of Jesus reaching out to those who were in such great need of His compassion and pardon.

Jesus didn't go along with the status quo of His day in regard to women, who, for all practical purposes back then, were invisible. He was governed by a higher standard, and His willingness to accept every-one equally got Him in trouble with the holy men of the times. Jesus defied the notion that any well-respected Jewish male did not publicly speak to a woman, even if she was his mother, his sister, or his wife.

He first displayed His openness to women (who were considered weak and unworthy) when he struck up a conversation with a Samari-tan woman by a well, as recorded in Luke, chapter 4. The facts that she was racially unacceptable to the Jews, had faulty religious beliefs, and had a history of divorce and immorality did not distract Jesus from her spiritually parched condition. He let her know that she had a bigger problem than where she was residing. She was perishing spiritually, and He was the only water that could quench her thirst. Although she was a blatant sinner, it was to her that Jesus first revealed Himself as the Mes-siah. Her encounter with Jesus was so deeply impacting that she left her water jar in the dust and ran into town to spread the news about this Man who knew so much. She, in essence, became His first missionary!

There was another woman, a prostitute no less, who anointed Jesus' feet with perfume, kissing them and wiping them with her hair. When a Pharisee chided Him for letting such a woman touch Him, Jesus responded by sharing a story about forgiveness. Then He turned to the woman and offered these words of love: "Your sins have been forgiven… Your faith has saved you; go in peace" (Luke 7:48,50). No doubt she went away changed forever!

Jesus didn't condemn a religiously "unclean" woman (the result of a 12-year hemorrhage) for reaching out to touch Him or His garment. Instead of responding angrily because her desperate act could have made Him ceremonially unclean, He declared in the presence of everyone in earshot, "Daughter, your faith has made you well; go in peace and be healed of your affliction" (Mark 5:34).

He didn't hesitate to take the hand of a 12-year-old dead girl although it was a violation of Jewish law, so He could give her back to her father alive and restored to health.

Each of these acts of kindness and mercy to broken souls reveal how Jesus smashed the rules and shattered the taboos of man-made righteousness. He often sent the religious establishment into a murderous rage by His words of love and forgiveness that threatened their way of life and rule. At every turn Jesus demonstrated that He lived by the greatest of all commandments—love. He didn't come to keep the Law; He came to fulfill it.

Who Is Without Sin?

Of all the women we've noted so far who were recipients of Jesus' marvelous acceptance and forgiveness, His lavish love is especially made clear in His interaction with a prostitute (see John 8). Many of us are familiar with this account of the infamous woman who was captured in the "very act of adultery." She was brought to Jesus by the church and civic leaders of that community to determine what punishment she should receive for her terrible sin. The Scriptures make it plain that

Jesus wasn't really being consulted because they wanted to know what they should do, but rather this sinful woman was being used as a snare to trap Jesus into doing something they could formally charge him with in the Jewish Council.

If He concurred with the Pharisees that Mosaic Law demanded she be killed, then they could accuse Him of being a hypocrite. Jesus was well-known for being a friend to those weighed down by sin. He made no attempt to hide His associations with the religious and socially unacceptable people of his day.

On the other hand, if Jesus asked for the woman to be shown mercy rather than judgment, He would be putting His opinion above the Law and making Himself greater than Moses. The men who brought the adulteress to Jesus were sure they had Him in an impossible situation. They couldn't lose.

To get a clearer picture of what was happening, let's consider the historical background related to Jesus' encounter with the accused woman. I believe it was obvious to Jesus that this scenario was a set-up. In order to stone a woman for the sin of adultery, there were specific criteria. There had to be two or three eyewitness who agreed on every detail of what happened. Catching a couple in a compromising situation was not enough to convict them. Those testifying against the couple had to observe the act. If there was any disagreement between witnesses, the case had to be dismissed.

This being true, where was the woman's partner in crime? According to Leviticus, the offending man must also be executed. Also, most pictorial accounts of this story portray the woman as an adult. However, it is more probable that the "woman" was really a teenage girl. By definition, to commit adultery, a woman had to be engaged or married and having intercourse with a man who was not her betrothed. An engaged woman was more likely to be somewhere around the age of 13 or 14. Also, because she was "caught in the act," she was probably only partially clothed, further humiliating her. I can only imagine the disgust Jesus felt when these men brought this frightened young girl to Him for the sole purpose of entrapment. Not only did these church leaders orchestrate such an evil plot, they used the Holy Scriptures to justify asking for her death.

The Pharisees demanded a response from Jesus regarding this adulteress. Jesus stooped down and wrote in the dirt with His finger. Don't you wish you could have been looking over His shoulder to see what He was writing? I do! Whatever it was, it must have been interesting. However, the men in the crowd continued to demand a response. Jesus answered their question with a challenge of His own: "He who is without sin among you, let him be the first to throw a stone at her" (John 8:7).

The Greek word used for the phrase "without sin" is very probing and exact. It implies that only those who had not committed the same sin were eligible to be the woman's judge. In our English language, we can easily misinterpret this phrase to mean "the one who is not perfect." To paraphrase Jesus' statement to the woman's accusers, "The one who is morally pure and has not committed adultery, you and you alone can throw the first stone." Evidently, not one of these men was morally innocent, for they dropped their stones of judgment and left.[1]

Then Jesus looked at the woman. His words must have been like a cool glass of water to one dying of thirst: "'Woman, where are they? Did no one condemn you?' She said, 'No one, Lord.' And Jesus said, 'I do not condemn you, either. Go. From now on sin no more.'"

There it is. The beautiful divine duet shown in God's Word once again, giving us the hope and instruction we need. God's part is to throw us the lifeline of forgiveness: "I do not condemn you." Our part is to confess our sins and repent of them: "Go and sin no more." The end result: Redemption! Like He did for the adulterous woman that day, Jesus did not come to judge and condemn us. He came to seek and to save those who are lost (Luke 19:10).

Silencing the Accuser

Having these accounts of women so beautifully touched by Christ gives us a distinct advantage when it comes to distinguishing between the true Forgiver and the condemning accuser. Christ's hands and heart are open to anyone seeking redemption. He reaches out to lift us up, and He does so without pointing a condemning finger. But like the cruel Pharisees who were pointing judgmental fingers at the woman caught in adultery, the accuser tries to magnify our failings and threatens to throw us in the dirt. Christ's voice covers us with love, speaks of pardon from sin, and offers us freedom. The accuser speaks and leaves us feeling exposed, guilt-ridden, and condemned.

With an understanding of the difference between the voices, what can we do if we hear the accuser? The only thing strong enough to resist the voice of guilt is the knowledge and confidence that our sins have been forgiven through Christ. Where do we find that kind of assurance? God's Word!

First John 1:9 tells us how we can be sure are sins are forgiven: "If we confess our sins, He is faithful and righteous to forgive us our sins and to cleanse us from all unrighteousness."

I have a graphic illustration of how extensive God's forgiveness is, but it's not for the faint of heart or weak of stomach. Imagine the worse case of intestinal influenza you've ever had. Can you feel your stomach gurgling and roiling? About the time you can't stand it anymore, the internal rumble decides its time to make its escape through the "south gate." The toilet bowl is now full. You gratefully reach for and push the little lever down that is mounted on the side of the commode. This movement activates the flushing mechanism in the toilet, and it does its very timely and wonderful job. Down, down, down the mess goes— out of sight, leaving only a memory in your mind of what happened. As gross as this is, my friend, it's a great picture of God's forgiveness.

The insides of our souls can churn with spiritual sicknesses such as bitterness, hatred, fear, jealousy, resentment, and the desire for revenge. When that "rumble" begins to happen, sooner or later our spirit will cry out for relief. The good news is there's a place we can dump the mess and have it whisked away. We confess our sins to God, and He, in His great mercy, pushes the lever on the tank of our lives and away goes the horrible, disgusting mess. He flushes it all away, never to be seen or dealt with again! Psalm 103:12 says, "As far as the east is from the west, so far has He removed our transgressions from us."

When we confess our sins, God takes care of them. They are gone forever. He will never remind us of our sin once it is confessed because it is "no more." If you're lying awake feeling guilty about something you did, say on graduation night, and you've already asked God for forgiveness, it is not God who is making you feel wretched! He's forgiven your sin and swept it away. Who you're hearing is the accuser, who tries to contradict God's forgiveness and turn you away from His love. And it's the same situation for a sin you did yesterday, as long as you confess, repent, and accept God's forgiveness.

What a shame when we allow the enemy of our souls to steal the truth about the forgiveness we have through Christ. When God says we're forgiven, we are forgiven!

I've met many people who said, "God might be able to forgive me for what I've done, but I can never forgive myself." These people are choosing to stay in bondage. They're essentially saying they are more holy and righteous than God. Think about this for a minute. If God can forgive a sin and loves us so much that He will do so through His grace and mercy, who are we to countermand His will and desire? Who are we to consider ourselves better judges than God the Almighty?

God's Word says, "If our heart does not condemns us, we have confidence before God" (1 John 3:21). When God says we are forgiven, that's that! We can do nothing to merit His mercy and His grace. We can only receive it and be grateful that He has deemed us acceptable in His sight because of what Jesus did for us.

Don't Fall for the Trick

Although God's grace abounds, we need to realize that there is a price to pay each time we violate God's principles. Colossians 3:25 warns, "He who does wrong will receive the consequence of the wrong which he has done, and that without partiality." For instance, you can be forgiven but still...

- be pregnant out of wedlock
- have AIDS

- deal with lack of trust in a marriage because of infidelity
- lose your job for embezzling
- damage someone's reputation because of gossip you shared
- lose your license due to driving under the influence of intoxicants
- go to jail for a crime you committed

Because there are indeed consequences to sin, one of Satan's best tools of trickery to push you into the mucky mire of guilt is to convince you that if you are truly forgiven, God would remove any consequences of the sin. Making the assumption that God's divine forgiveness automatically cancels out any unwanted side effects of our sins makes us unnecessarily vulnerable to the voice of the accuser.

The laws of planting and harvesting are easily seen in our physical world. We all know that when we plant a field of corn, we don't gather a crop of wheat. The same principle of sowing and reaping can be applied to spiritual laws. When we sow seeds of deceit and immorality, we are bound to reap a harvest of distrust and guilt.

· · · · ·

God wants us to focus on what *He* has done for us, while Satan wants us to focus on what *we* have done.

· · · · ·

There are two truths that may seem on the surface to be hard to reconcile, and yet they are completely compatible in God's plan. The first truth is fundamental: God's complete forgiveness of our sins and His limitless love are quickly and lavishly offered to a sinful world (John 3:16). But just as sure as God's love is indisputable, the second truth stands unashamed and unchallenged. It is best described this way: "Do not be deceived, God is not mocked; for whatever a man sows, this he will also reap. For the one who sows to his own flesh will from the flesh reap corruption, but the one who sows to the Spirit will from the Spirit reap eternal life" (Galatians 6:7-8).

Even though our sinful actions may set into motion consequences that are painful and far-reaching, we shouldn't listen to the devilish voice of the accuser as he strives to convince us that God's forgiveness is incomplete because we are suffering the consequences of our actions.

Instead of falling for such deceit, remember that God's forgiveness is unconditional. He offers extravagant grace, unmerited mercy, and limitless love even in the presence of the painful consequences we experience. The results of sin can be a reminder of His grace, not His judgment. And what does that produce? Joy! Armed with this truth, the next time the voice of the accuser comes and attempts to sicken you with reminders of past sins, remind him that you serve Christ, and He forgives your every sin, even the most heinous. And He'll continue to do so because He is "the same yesterday and today and forever" (Hebrews 13:8). And even though you are dealing with the result of your transgression, the sin itself has been flushed away. God wants us to focus on what *He* has done for us, while Satan wants us to focus on what *we* have done.

To add to your arsenal of biblical truths about God's forgiveness, why not memorize these biblical passages that can be used to silence the accuser?

Ephesians 2:1,4-5: "You were dead in your trespasses and sins…But God, being rich in mercy, because of His great love with which He loved us, even when we were dead in our transgressions, made us alive together with Christ (by grace you have been saved)."

Psalm 32:1-5: "How blessed is he whose transgression is forgiven, whose sin is covered! How blessed is the man to whom the LORD does not impute iniquity, and in whose spirit there is no deceit! When I kept silent about my sin, my body wasted away through my groaning all day long. For day and night Your hand was heavy upon me; my vitality was drained away as with the fever heat of summer. Selah. I acknowledged my sin to You, and my iniquity I did not hide; 'I said I will confess my transgressions to the LORD'; and You forgave the guilt of my sin."

2 Corinthians 7:9-10: "I now rejoice, not that you were made sorrowful, but that you were made sorrowful to the point of repentance;

for you were made sorrowful according to the will of God, so that you might not suffer loss in anything through us. For the sorrow that is according to the will of God produces a repentance without regret, leading to salvation, but the sorrow of the world produces death."

Ephesians 1:7: "In Him we have redemption through His blood, the forgiveness of our trespasses, according to the riches of His grace."

Colossians 2:13-14: "When you were dead in your transgressions and the uncircumcision of your flesh, He made you alive together with Him, having forgiven us all our transgressions, having canceled out the certificate of debt consisting of decrees against us, which was hostile to us; and He has taken it out of the way, having nailed it to the cross."

6

Choosing Whose Voice You'll Listen To

We are more than what we have done,
and we are more than what has been done to us.

ANNIE CHAPMAN

When the women's conference where I was speaking broke for lunch, a lady walked up to me with drooped shoulders. Standing at my side she quietly told her secret without lifting her gaze from the floor.

"I have never told anyone this before, but when I was 20 years old, I had an abortion. I am now 80, and I have suffered every day of my life from that terrible choice. The sin of abortion has defined who I am, and it has become a horrible source of shame."

As she spoke in her hushed and humble tone my heart ached with compassion and sorrow for this precious woman. I quietly responded, "Did you ever ask God to forgive you?"

With a sudden upward jerk of her head, she looked me straight in the eyes and emphatically said, "A million times."

Instantly I was filled with sad anger at the damage that sin does to God's creation. I said, "That mean old devil! He has been tormenting you for 60 years for something God forgave and chose to forget. It's time for you to let yourself off the hook. You can't unscramble eggs, so what's done is done. But, dear woman, you dare not carry the shame of that sin one moment longer. God isn't mad at you. He loves you. That's the good news of what Jesus did on the cross."

As she listened to what I was saying, a smile crept across the elderly woman's face. I could see relief flood her eyes. Slowly she turned to join her lunch buddies, who were waiting for her at the back of the room. I noticed she walked more upright, more confident, and I knew a terrible load had been lifted off her heart and shoulders.

This is what an encounter with Jesus brings to those who are willing to embrace the truth of His forgiveness! When we carry our sins, He feels sorrow and pain because we aren't listening to Him or accepting His forgiveness. In the words of the elderly woman, too often we allow *what we have done to define who we are.* That sad condition is called shame.

Silencing Shame

The voice of the accuser is always ready to remind us of the sins we've committed. And when we fail to understand and embrace the forgiveness God has provided, we make ourselves even more vulnerable to the accuser's use of shame. What does shame's voice sound like? It's rather easy to identify because it always calls us names and attaches labels to us:

- You are so *stupid.* Why did you trust that person? You should have known better.

- You're a *worthless piece of trash.* You'll never change. You should just give up.

- You're *hopelessly poor and uneducated.* That's all you'll ever be. It's crazy to think about going back to school. Why try to be more than you are?

- You're a *bad husband.* Your wife would have been better off marrying that guy she was dating when she met you. You don't make enough money, and you're at work all the time. Your family would be better off without you.

- You're a *bad wife.* You deserve what happened. No wonder your husband ran off with that other woman. And the reason he beat you is because you provoked him. No one could be happy with you. The divorce is your fault.

- You're a *murderer.* How could God ever use someone who had an abortion and killed her own baby?

- You're a *drunk,* and you'll always be one. Your daddy, your granddaddy, your granddaddy's daddy—all the men in your family were alcoholics…You'll never amount to anything.

- You're a *hypocrite.* You should quit going to church. You never pray or read your Bible. And if the people at your church really knew what you're like, they'd kick you out.

- You're a *bad mother.* You never know where your kids are. They are going to grow up and hate you, just like you hated your mother. The children would be better off with a different mom.

There is no end to the names and cruel labels the voice of shame uses against us. What's worse, that awful voice is especially merciless to those who deal with the sad effects of things that happened to them over which they had no control, such as children who have been sexually abused. To these desperate ones God wants to give them back their dignity and comfort—if they'll only listen to His voice of redemption. My favorite story on this point comes from the life of Mary Ann Bird. Here's what she wrote:

> I grew up knowing I was different, and I hated it. I was born with a cleft palate, and when I started school, my classmates made it clear to me how I looked to others: a little girl with a misshapen lip, crooked nose, lopsided teeth, and garbled speech.
>
> When schoolmates asked, "What happened to your lip?" I'd tell them I'd fallen and cut it on a piece of glass. Somehow it seemed more acceptable to have suffered an accident than to have been born different. I was convinced that no one outside my family could love me.
>
> There was, however, a teacher in the second grade whom

we all adored—Mrs. Leonard. She was short, round, happy—a sparkling lady.

Annually we had a hearing test…Mrs. Leonard gave the test to everyone in the class, and finally it was my turn. I knew from past years that as we stood against the door and covered one ear, the teacher sitting at her desk would whisper something, and we would have to repeat it back—things like "The sky is blue" or "Do you have new shoes?" I waited there for words that God must have put into her mouth, those seven words that changed my life. Mrs. Leonard said in her whisper, "I wish you were my little girl."[1]

All of us have been deformed by sin in some way as a result of living in this fallen world. By our own failings and the faults of others, we are wounded, scarred people. The voice of shame sneers its malicious taunts constantly: "You're no good," "No one loves you," and "You'll never change."

· · · · · ·
Choosing to listen to what God says about
you and your circumstance will make all
the difference in your happiness.
· · · · · ·

Take courage! There is another voice that is speaking to us constantly as well. The voice of the sweet Holy Spirit comes to us despite our poverty of soul, brokenness of body, and torment of spirit. He speaks softly into our ears, whispering His loving hope into our spirits: "I want you to be my little girl" or "I want you to be my little boy." Which voice are you going to listen to and take to heart?

The voice of shame may argue against the comforting words of the Holy Spirit. You may even "hear" thoughts such as "But, Lord, don't you know what I've done? Do I have to tell you how badly I've messed up? I'm not sure you can forgive someone like me." My friend, please resist allowing that voice to demean what Jesus has done on the cross for you! Understand that only God's Word is strong enough to silence the pitiless voice of shame. Choosing to listen to what God says about you and your circumstance will make all the difference in your happiness. To help you replace the voice of shame with God's wisdom and promises, remember these passages.

Isaiah 54:4: "Fear not, for you will not be put to shame; and do not feel humiliated, for you will not be disgraced; but you will forget the shame of your youth, and the reproach of your widowhood you will remember no more."

Do you get the scope of this passage? The shame from as far back as when you were very young and all the way to your old age is removed! Isn't this great news?

Hebrews 4:14-16 NKJV: "Seeing then that we have a great High Priest who has passed through the heavens, Jesus the Son of God, let us hold fast our confession. For we do not have a High Priest who cannot sympathize with our weaknesses, but was in all points tempted as we are, yet without sin. Let us therefore come boldly to the throne of grace, that we may obtain mercy and find grace to help in time of need."

Psalm 31:16-17: "Make Your face to shine upon Your servant; save me in Your lovingkindness. Let me not be put to shame, O LORD, for I call upon You."

Romans 4:7-8: "Blessed are those whose lawless deeds have been forgiven, and whose sins have been covered. Blessed is the man whose sin the Lord will not take into account."

Isaiah 61:4,7: "Then they will rebuild the ancient ruins, they will raise up the former devastations; and they will repair the ruined cities, the desolations of many generations...Instead of your shame you will have a double portion, and instead of humiliation they will shout for joy over their portion."

Joel 2:25-27: "I will make up to you for the years that the swarming locust has eaten, the creeping locust, the stripping locust, and the gnawing locust, My great army which I sent among you. You will have plenty to eat and be satisfied and praise the name of the LORD your God, who has dealt wondrously with you; then My people will never be put to shame. Thus you will know that I am in the midst of Israel, and that I am the LORD your God, and there is no other; and My people will never be put to shame."

Romans 8:1: "There is now no condemnation for those who are in Christ Jesus."

Truth vs. Fact

The key to whether we will succumb to the voice of shame or submit to the wooing and soothing counsel of the Holy Spirit is our willingness to embrace the truth over shame's glaring spotlight on the old facts. The truths that we have repented of our sins and accepted Christ's sacrifice means we are redeemed by Him. And this trumps any condemning facts from the past. Some of us may have histories that are more colorfully painted than others, but one thing is for sure, none of us have an entirely clean canvas. The past doesn't matter.

There are plenty of people mentioned in the Bible who testify to God's amazing ability and willingness to paint beautiful pictures over smudged canvases that have been redeemed in Him. For example, the great patriarch Abraham lied about his marriage to Sarah, but God made him the father of many nations. David sinned with Bathsheba and had her husband murdered, yet he was called the "apple of God's eye." Peter denied Christ three times yet God used him mightily in spreading the gospel and establishing the church. Paul severely persecuted Christians yet God used him to win many to Christ. With these few reminders of God's willingness to use souls who were surely ongoing targets of Satan's barbs of shame, I hope you are encouraged that He will deliver you and use your life for His glory as well.

Nothing Is Hidden

From time to time my thoughts return to that sweet lady at the conference who had the terribly big secret about having an abortion when she was young. I recall when she first came up to talk to me. I see her standing there in front of the church, bowed down not in glorious worship but in bitter shame. Thankfully, my thoughts always end with the joyful look of relief on her face as she realized God had really forgiven her and He wasn't mad at her.

While I rejoice with this woman who found freedom, my heart breaks for others who gather with believers yet haven't realized they are truly forgiven so they haven't experienced the same life-changing liberty. If this is true for you, I offer good news. This lyric, written by my husband, Steve, is specifically for those who feel they cannot openly reveal their battle with shame:

Unspoken Request

The preacher got up; he said, "Stand to your feet!
We'll start with a prayer, if you have a need.
Let it be heard; saints, let it be known,
We're family here; you're not alone."

But that's when he saw her in the back of the church,
Her sadness and silence cried out the hurt.
But the kind shepherd knew just what to say,
"I need to know before we pray…

An unspoken request—
Does anybody have one here tonight?
Did you come with a burden you can't share, a need in
your life?
Just lift up your hand to the one who can give you rest.
Child, have no fear; our God can hear
An unspoken request."

"Well," the preacher whispered as she raised her hand,
"Sweet Holy Spirit come by her and stand."
And when her tears started flowin'
He had no doubt
That in the throne room of heaven her secret was out.[2]

God sees your heart and longs for you to walk out from under such sin weight. I pray that He will speak to you right now and comfort you with His presence. Receive the renewed hope He offers and places in the deepest regions of your heart. Open up to Him at this moment and ask Him to help you resist the voice of shame and silence the enemy's relentless attack. Don't surrender your peace through Jesus Christ to the enemy. Your heavenly Father says to you, "I want you to be My child."

7

Evicting Fear, Doubt, and Despair

He who fears God need fear nothing else,
and he who fears not God
needs to fear everything else.

Author unknown

I once heard a story about a little boy who was confronted every morning on his way to school by an oversized classmate who demanded a nickel. Day after day the young man reluctantly forked over his five cents. Finally the tormented kid decided enough was enough.

Taking the phone book in hand he looked up the number for a local karate class. He decided he was going to confront the bully—saving his money and his dignity. The instructor conducting the self-defense class informed the boy that although he could teach him how to fight the thug, there were some things he would have to do. He would have to commit to attending the classes, faithfully practice the defensive moves, and pay the required fee per session. After carefully considering the proposed responsibilities he would have to assume, the kid replied, "It would be cheaper to pay the nickel."[1]

How many of us have decided that it's easier to pay the bully than to discover and implement what it takes to resist the voices that steal our joy and rob our peace? No doubt, there is a price that must be paid; however, the cost is well worth the benefit of being free.

God-given, Healthy Fear

The ability to feel emotions is God-given. A simple definition of "emotion" is how we react to a circumstance or a situation. For instance, feeling fearful when we are placed in a vulnerable situation is one reaction God has given us to sense danger and protect ourselves. Our senses are rightly put on alert when we are approached by a large, unfamiliar dog or a blaring tornado warning splits the silence. If we hear a window breaking in the middle of the night we are properly goaded to grab the phone and call for help. Being fearful in a threatening situation is a natural reaction and an accurate response.

Fear is also appropriate when the situation is merely *perceived* as threatening. Imagine walking along a wooded trail. In the distance you observe a large bear feeding among the blackberry bushes. The rush of adrenalin and the knowledge that you are no match for the burly beast causes you to take action. You leave the area. Fear of the bear has served you well—and may well have saved your life.

• • • • •

When thoughts and feelings are given
more power in our lives than our trust
in God, we must take steps to bring our
emotions back under God's authority.

• • • • •

So when do emotions cross the line and become negative? And do strong emotions cross the healthy line? The strength of the emotion is not what causes a spiritual problem. It's when we give emotions controlling power over our lives that they become "bullies" that must be defeated. Let's use the previous examples of fear to explore when emotions become spiritual liabilities.

When we exchange our natural, healthy reluctance to face an unfamiliar large dog for being terrified of any critter with fur and paws, our fear has taken on a renegade quality. Fear has become an ungodly vehicle that takes us to a place we should not go. The moment we recognize our fears have become lofty and raised themselves above the knowledge and wisdom of God—the moment they try to take control—that's when we must take them captive and resist the voice of fear.

When we have replaced a legitimate fear of a destructive tornado and are unable to go outside on sunny days because we are afraid of the possibility of bad weather, we have surrendered our God-given peace for the voice of fear. When thoughts and feelings are given more power in our lives than our trust in God, we must take steps to bring our emotions back under God's authority.

Living in a Scary World

For as long as I can remember, I've been more apt to reject fear than to entertain it. While I've had an occasional bout with genuine fear during my early years, my take-charge personality has helped me overcome negative encounters that might otherwise have plagued me. Sudden run-ins on the farm where I grew up with unfriendly critters like snakes, bobcats, bees, and even rabid dogs didn't rattle me much. I found that yelling and wildly swinging clubs made of whatever I could reach were good responses to ward off attacks and fear. My bent toward fearlessness continued into my teen years, which was made especially evident when I left home at 17.

I'll not forget when, as a dairy farmer's daughter, I made the decision to leave the country and move to the Windy City. Chicago was a huge metropolis and a big change. The dramatic move from Southside, West Virginia to the southside of Chicago Avenue was overwhelming and filled with challenges. However, instead of being afraid of my new surroundings, I was enthralled with them.

Those early days of being on my own were filled with many firsts that should have given me pause or even terrified me. The day I left home I experienced my first flight on an airplane. After I arrived at O'Hare International Airport, I took my first ride on a large city bus. After being dropped off in the middle of Chicago's downtown Loop, I hailed my first taxi that took me to Moody Bible Institute, where I was enrolled for the fall semester. With my childlike faith that God had brought me to that place and the assurance that He was going to take care of me, I stood on the sidewalk looking at the school entry that is called "The Arch." I had one suitcase and one paper sack of possessions for this new chapter in my life. I was completely free from fear and filled with faith. And I'm happy to report that all went well during my Chicago years.

My fearlessness went with me when I graduated and moved to Philadelphia to be part of Teen Haven, a ministry under the leadership of Reverend Bill Drury. We were dedicated to taking the message of Christ's gospel to the streets of the City of Brotherly Love. I, along with the staff at the North Broad Street center, worked in the inner city teaching children to read and conducting Bible studies in local neighborhoods and projects. God's grace once again kept me strong and courageous as I walked along the streets and visited in the homes of those who lived around our center.

My propensity for exerting a persona of bravery was challenged, however. On one occasion I was surrounded by a gang of young men who didn't appreciate an outsider coming into their territory to influence the young people of the neighborhood toward God. As they circled and taunted me with threats, I kept my eyes fixed straight ahead and kept walking. I don't know who was more surprised when they parted their ranks and let me walk through their circle and continue down the street.

During my time at Teen Haven, I served as a camp counselor for a group of young girls who were members of a notorious gang. The leader of the girls was a rather large young lady who decided she didn't like me telling her what to do. She got in my face and told me she was going to kill me. Without blinking, I faced her down. What she didn't realize was that growing up on a dairy farm I routinely handled angry bulls that didn't want to go into the barn and stubborn cows that didn't want to be milked. As far as I was concerned she was just a bullette who needed to be corralled. When she saw that I was not fazed by her intimidation, she backed down. Although we never became fast friends, the two of us established a truce based on mutual respect.

How I dealt with these intimidating situations without "freaking out," as we said in the 70s, remains a mystery. Perhaps my faith in God was my strength…or it may be that I proceeded in ignorant bliss and God, in His great mercy, sent angels to take care of me (I lean toward the latter explanation). I am grateful that fear wasn't a debilitating issue during those years. Over the years my predisposition for forging ahead in difficult situations has been tempered.

The Concert Problem

Steve and I were putting on a concert in a large church in Illinois. During the concert, which was being broadcast live over the radio, it was discovered that a woman had brought a loaded revolver into the sanctuary where we were singing. According to one of the church ushers after the concert, the woman had come to the event with the intention of standing up in the middle of the crowd and killing herself. Thankfully, at the end of the evening performance, the lady had given the gun to one of the ushers at the door and told him she'd changed her mind. She reported that something she'd heard that night made her want to go on living.

Although the evening didn't end tragically, I developed an apprehension about being on stage in front of a large crowd.

Later that year Steve and I were performing at a fund-raiser for a crisis pregnancy center in Michigan. While we were presenting our concert, a lady stood up and began screaming at me. The large crowd immediately turned its attention toward the hysterical woman. Since I was wrapping up an introduction to our next song, "The Highchair," it took me a moment to understand what was happening. Part of the introduction was a challenge to consider the importance of rearing our own children and giving our kids the best of our time and effort. What I'd said apparently didn't sit well with the lady, who seemed to disagree with our position on family issues.

After her rant about how horrible men are, how women have to do all the work, and how she loved her job and didn't want to stay home with her children, the lady ran out of the auditorium. As she fled, I suddenly heard the voice of fear speaking loud and clear: "This time that woman yelled at you, but the next time it happens, someone will shoot you!"

Raw fear filled my heart. The blood began to pound in my ears, and I felt myself sway as my equilibrium gave way to dizziness. I fought to stay upright. Right there, in front of all those people, I experienced a full-blown, spiritual panic attack. With God's help, I managed to pull myself together enough to get through the rest of the evening.

We later learned the woman had wandered into the concert by mistake. She thought she was supporting a pro-abortion rally instead of attending a right-to-life gathering.

In the months that followed, each time Steve and I performed a concert and we'd get to the song "The Highchair," I would experience the same knee-buckling, head-spinning, heart-thumping anxiety. This ongoing and annoying battle with the voice of fear could only be won with one weapon: God's Word. I turned to Psalm 33:16-19 for strength and comfort:

> The king is not saved by a mighty army; a warrior is not delivered by great strength. A horse is a false hope for victory; nor does it deliver anyone by its great strength. Behold, the eye of the LORD is on those who fear Him, on those who hope for His lovingkindness, to deliver their soul from death and to keep them alive in famine.

This passage spoke to me and quieted the voice of fear because it made me ask an important question: Who did I fear? Would I entertain an unhealthy fear of man (or a ranting, gun-toting woman) or was I going to choose a healthy reverence (fear) for God? I knew I could trust God to deliver me from danger. So by continually turning to Him and using His Word for courage, I found victory that continues to this day.

Fear-free Flying

After the attacks on the United States by Islamic terrorists on September 11, 2001, like many people I was terrified to fly on airplanes.

Steve and I had returned from the East Coast just one day before the terrorists used four passenger jets as missiles to attack the heart and soul of America. It was bone-chilling to realize that had their plan been implemented 24 hours earlier, Steve and I might have been among the causalities of that act of terrorism. After our perceived close call, flying was the last thing I wanted to do. However, as soon as the airports were reopened, Steve and I were scheduled to give a concert in Detroit, Michigan…and we had to fly to get there on time.

As I was preparing for the trip, I found myself nearly immobilized by terror. The thought of stepping onboard any aircraft sent me into a fit of dry heaves. What was I going to do? The voice of fear drowned out all my positive thinking as my mind was saturated by the weeklong images of crumpling buildings, twisted metal, and people jumping out of high-rise windows. My ears rang from the mournful laments of families who had lost their loved ones, and my eyes burned from so many tears that flowed as I watched the smoke belch out of the hole where once stood the majestic Twin Towers of New York City.

I realized there was no way I could think my way out of this debilitating phobia. And my escalating fear of flying was the vehicle Satan was using to gain control over me. I concluded that if I didn't get a grip on what I was allowing to feed my mind I was going to be grounded forever. To fight back I took the bully by the horns, so to speak. I went to the only source stronger than my fear: God's Word. I felt a bit like Queen Esther when she faced the choice between boldly doing what she knew God wanted her to do and facing possible death if her husband, the king, was affronted by her appearing unannounced before him. Esther declared, "If I perish, I perish" (Esther 4:16). I decided that I too would rather go down trusting God than living outside of His pleasure.

I frantically searched through the Bible for verses that might silence my relentless foe. Like a drowning woman going down into the deep, dark waters for the third time, I grabbed the lifeline and caught hold of the truths of God. One particular passage provided the rope I needed to pull myself (with God's help!) out of the water. Joshua 1:8-9 says,

This book of the law shall not depart from your mouth, but you shall meditate on it day and night, so that you may be careful to do according to all that is written in it; for then you will make your way prosperous, and then you will have success. Have I not commanded you? Be strong and courageous! Do not tremble or be dismayed, for the LORD your God is with you wherever you go.

On the day we were scheduled to fly to Detroit, I wrote those precious words in Joshua on a piece of paper and put them right next to my body and held it in place with the belt I was wearing. When the fear would creep into my heart and the voice of dread whispered, I slid my hand under my belt and touched the words from God I'd written down. When I did that, the enemy would flee and my confidence would return. I used this method countless times on that flight and the many more that followed.

Returning to the airways taught me a great lesson. As I filled my mind with God's Word, there was no room left for fear, doubt, or despair. I know this because of the confidence and support I experienced the morning I got on the airplane with Joshua 1:8-9 tucked in my heart...and under my belt! I knew I couldn't eliminate the potential of danger nor could I forget what had happened so recently, but I could replace those devastating thoughts and images with the knowledge that nothing can touch me that does not first come through the filter of God's strong and mighty hand.

How are you doing with fear? Are you dealing with a "screamer" who is trying to intimidate or frighten you? Are you facing a "9/11" situation and coming up short on bravery? I encourage you to read this chapter as many times as you need to so that God's Word and His wisdom will fill your heart.

More Encouragement from God's Word

Here are some additional scriptures I've leaned on through the years when the voice of fear whispers or yells in my ear. Take note of how the "divine duet" is revealed in each one and how the "hearing and do-ing" of these verses can produce victory over the nagging "what ifs" that attempt to rob us of our faith.

John 14:27 NIV: "Peace I leave with you; my peace I give you. I do not give to you as the world gives. Do not let your hearts be troubled and do not be afraid."

Matthew 8:25-26 NIV: "The disciples went and woke him, saying, 'Lord, save us! We're going to drown!' He replied, 'You of little faith, why are you so afraid?' Then he got up and rebuked the winds and the waves, and it was completely calm."

Acts 18:9-11 NIV: "One night the Lord spoke to Paul in a vision: 'Do not be afraid; keep on speaking, do not be silent. For I am with you, and no one is going to attack and harm you, because I have many peo-ple in this city.' So Paul stayed for a year and a half, teaching them the word of God."

Isaiah 12:2: "Behold, God is my salvation, I will trust and not be afraid; for the LORD GOD is my strength and song, and He has become my salvation." Notice the progression: God *is* our salvation, but after we actively choose faith over fear, God *becomes* our salvation.

Psalm 56:1-4: "Be gracious to me, O God, for man has trampled upon me; fighting all day long he oppresses me. My foes have tram-pled upon me all day long, for they are many who fight proudly against me. When I am afraid, I will put my trust in You. In God, whose word I praise, in God I put my trust; I shall not be afraid. What can mere man do to me?"

David declares his faith in God and dependence upon His Word even in the face of great peril and fear. This psalm was written when David sought refuge in the city of Gath, which was the hometown of Goliath, the notorious giant David toppled when he was younger. Fleeing the attacks of King Saul, David found himself alone in a hos-tile city, without food, without a weapon, and without his protective army (1 Samuel 21–22). David cried out to God, showing us that our choice is between fear and trust.

Psalm 121: "I will lift up my eyes to the mountains; from where shall my help come? My help comes from the LORD, who made heaven and earth. He will not allow your foot to slip; He who keeps you will not slumber. Behold, He who keeps Israel will neither slumber nor sleep.

"The LORD is your keeper; the LORD is your shade on your right hand. The sun will not smite you by day, nor the moon by night. The LORD will protect you from all evil; He will keep your soul. The LORD will guard your going out and your coming in from this time forth and forever."

Psalm 4:6-8: "Many are saying, 'Who can show us any good?' Lift up the light of Your countenance upon us, O LORD! You have put gladness in my heart, more than when their grain and new wine abound. In peace I will both lie down and sleep, for you alone, O LORD, make me to dwell in safety."

Isaiah 43:1-3: "Do not fear, for I have redeemed you; I have called you by name; you are Mine! When you pass through the waters, I will be with you; and through the rivers, they will not overflow you. When you walk through the fire, you will not be scorched, nor will the flame burn you. For I am the LORD your God, the Holy One of Israel, your Savior."

Psalm 91:11: "He will give His angels charge concerning you, to guard you in all your ways."

8

Refusing to Feel Discouraged

*Discouragement is to the soul what
cancer is to the body.*

ANNIE CHAPMAN

One of my all-time favorite movies is Frank Capra's *It's a Wonderful Life*. In the opening scene we hear George Bailey's family and friends lifting him up in prayer. The angel, Clarence (who was yet to get his wings), is sent to earth to help George (the main character).

The head angel informs Clarence that a man on earth needs help. Clarence asks if the man is sick.

And the head angel says it's even worse—the man is discouraged. And that at 10:45 the man will contemplate throwing away God's greatest gift—his life.

Clarence responds, saying he'd better hurry because he only has an hour to get ready.

George Bailey is a great illustration of what happens when people get discouraged.

When our children were small, Steve and I bought them a ball toy. It had a wall-mounted square of Velcro loop cloth and several little colored balls covered with Velcro hook material. Our family had a lot of fun throwing the balls at the wall and watching them stick to the square. One day while playing with the kids, it occurred to me that the game was a good picture of what happens to the human heart when cutting remarks are hurled at it. They seem to stick. Except the result is much worse because, unlike the little toy balls that were easily pulled off, mean-spirited words are much, much harder to remove.

Not only are words of discouragement difficult to forget, the long-term effects are undeniably significant. "Sticks and stones may break my bones, but words can never hurt me" is a folk saying (circa 1894) that the devil loves to propagate because it's not true and is used to cover up hurt, which can then fester and lead to discouragement. Yes, sticks and stones can break bones, but hurtful words break hearts. And have you noticed that it seems to take a hundred or more affirmations ("You're terrific!") to counteract one destructive phrase ("You're an idiot").

Poisonous verbal spears impact our spirits. There are many stories that relate how people get so discouraged that they commit suicide. Later we usually discover that such drastic measures were in response to relentless echoes of discouragement in their minds, such as "you're useless," "nobody likes you," and "you're a disappointment." But even when discouragement isn't this severe, it can have a permanent, negative impact on us. Steve and I will never forget the morning we were on the receiving end of words that hurt. While they didn't threaten our will to live, they tampered with the work we feel God has called us to do.

We were invited to conduct a marriage seminar weekend for a church in a small town. We did extensive preparation for the weekend and were excited to share information and ideas that would help build up marriages and families. Our primary goal was to encourage couples to make Christ the center of their homes.

Upon our arrival at the church, we were introduced to the senior pastor. He was friendly, and we enjoyed a brief conversation before the conference started. We were told he would be serving as the emcee. All was going well until the time came for our introduction. As the senior pastor spoke, it quickly became apparent that there had been a miscommunication between the staff heading up the marriage seminar and the pastor. He welcomed all the couples in attendance and then announced that the marriage seminar would begin that evening.

That would have been fine, except the committee in charge of the event didn't want us to start teaching on marriage until the next morning for the sake of the couples who couldn't make it that night. They'd asked us to give a more general, lighthearted presentation about family and parenting. With a sinking feeling in our stomachs we listened and realized our presentation wasn't going to match his description.

In confusion we rose from our seats and headed to the podium. As Steve adjusted his guitar strap on his shoulders he leaned over and whispered to me, "It's too late to change the set list for the sound and video technicians so let's do what we were originally asked to do." I was so flustered that it didn't dawn on me to suggest that we tell the audience that the teachings specifically about marriage would begin the next day. So we continued with the planners' original agenda. In spite of our mental chaos, the opening session seemed to connect well with the group.

That is, except for one important person. The next morning before the session began, the senior pastor again got up to address the couples. He explained what time we would break for lunch and the location of child-care and restrooms. He ended his remarks with a prayer, asking God's blessing on the days activities. As I recall, his prayer went something like this: "Dear Lord, You know that last night was a bit of a disappointment. It wasn't what we thought it would be. Although the session was light on content, we have greater hopes for today."

As we listened to the pastor speak to God, Steve was holding my hand. I felt his fingers tighten on mine. I've known Steve long enough to know by the way he was squeezing my hand that he was silently thinking, "Say what?" I snuck a peak at Steve and his bowed face had turned an angry red. I leaned over and whispered, "Suck it up, Bubba. We're here for these couples, and we don't want to disappoint the people who worked hard on this weekend."

Drawing on all the professionalism we could muster, we walked to the microphones and began the marriage seminar. We tried hard to conceal our feelings of doubt about our place at the podium, but we wondered if our bewilderment was visible.

We were so discouraged—actually devastated is a better description—by the comments that were directed to us under the mask of prayer. Neither of us had ever felt more emotionally deflated.

Later that evening, in the sanctuary of our hotel room, we hashed out the comments the pastor had made. We talked a long time, and then we knew we needed to get some sleep to be ready for the next day's teachings and services. As we readied for bed, I said, "Steve, it seems to me that the pastor accomplished in one day what the devil has not been able to do in more than 34 years. He has us questioning what we're doing and thinking about quitting."

We climbed into bed, and Steve agreed with my comment. He turned the light out. It wasn't easy to get to sleep that evening. Drifting off is hard to do when wolves are being counted instead of sheep.

The sting of discouragement didn't go away immediately. When we climbed onboard the airplane that was to take us back to Tennessee, we were still talking about it. The voice of discouragement echoed loudly in our heads for a long time. (And if it's occurred to you that sharing this story indicates that we still deal with the residual effects of that instance of hurt and misunderstanding, you'd be correct.)

While it was helpful to confess to each other that we had allowed our egos to be unnecessarily fragile, there was another level of recovery that was important to reach. When we realized that the enemy of our souls had taken the pastor's publicly spoken disappointment in our work and was using it to spiritually and emotionally browbeat us, we took affirmative steps to silence his voice of discouragement. We were able to regain our footing and continue to minister through music and teaching.

Perhaps you too have experienced moments or even seasons of discouragement that have left you wanting to give up. As I share the steps Steve and I took to find wholeness, contentment, and renewed confidence in knowing God's call on our lives, I hope you will discover insights into what you can do in your life to hush the enemy and his discouraging words.

Fill Your Mind with Truth

As Steve and I fought to keep from emotionally drowning in the pastor's demeaning comments, we reminded each other that the material (spoken and sung) we'd presented at the conference had been effective in our other conferences, and that the information was probably just as effective at the last event. This wasn't much comfort because we both realized that being defensive was really an attempt to justify ourselves, to elevate ourselves, to use pride from previous accomplishments to soothe our souls.

Next we hazarded guesses about what personal issues the senior pastor had that caused us to unknowingly "push his buttons" and make him feel uncomfortable. Then we could dismiss his remarks as vengeful. That idea didn't help because we soon realized we were being judgmental and looking for excuses.

Then we decided we needed to come to grips with the pastor's comments and consider them, using them as motivation to closely examine the material we presented to see if it could be improved. That helped somewhat, but our souls still ached.

Finally, we both agreed we would find the best comfort and encouragement in God's Word. Hebrews 4:12 tells us that His Word "is living and active and sharper than a two-edged sword." We needed an arsenal of spiritual weapons to use against the constant barrage of negativity that kept invading our peace and confidence. We also drew on the following powerful verses for strength, and I know they'll help you too.

Philippians 4:8-9: "Whatever is true, whatever is honorable, whatever is right, whatever is pure, whatever is lovely, whatever is of good repute, if there is any excellence and if anything worthy of praise, dwell on these things. The things you have learned and received and heard and seen in me, practice these things, and the God of peace will be with you."

Romans 5:1-5: "Therefore, having been justified by faith, we have peace with God through our Lord Jesus Christ, through whom also we have obtained our introduction by faith into this grace in which we stand; and we exult in hope of the glory of God. And not only this, but we also exult in our tribulations, knowing that tribulation brings about perseverance; and perseverance, proven character; and proven character, hope; and hope does not disappoint, because the love of God has been poured out within our hearts through the Holy Spirit who was given to us."

Lamentations 3:19-26: "Remember my affliction and my wandering, the wormwood and bitterness. Surely my soul remembers and is bowed down within me. This I recall to my mind, therefore I have hope. The LORD's lovingkindnesses indeed never cease, for His compassions never fail. They are new every morning; great is Your faithfulness. 'The LORD is my portion,' says my soul. 'Therefore I have hope in Him.' The LORD is good to those who wait for Him, to the person who seeks Him. It is good that he waits silently for the salvation of the LORD."

2 Corinthians 4:6-10: "For God, who said, 'Light shall shine out of darkness,' is the One who has shone in our hearts to give the Light of the knowledge of the glory of God in the face of Christ. But we have this treasure in earthen vessels, so that the surpassing greatness of the power will be of God and not from ourselves; we are afflicted in every way, but not crushed; perplexed, but not despairing; persecuted, but not forsaken; struck down, but not destroyed; always carrying about in the body the dying of Jesus, so that the life of Jesus also may be manifested in our body."

1 Peter 2:9: "You are a chosen race, a royal priesthood, a holy nation, a people for God's own possession, so that you may proclaim the excellencies of Him who has called you out of darkness into His marvelous light; for you once were not a people, but now you are the people of God; you had not received mercy, but now you have received mercy."

Spend Time with Encouraging People

Surrounding yourself with positive, encouraging people will help you see the roses instead of the thorns of life. People who lift you up will help you see the beautiful sunset instead of approaching darkness.

One of the most positive people I've met is my mother-in-law, Lillian Chapman. Although she has suffered with recurring back pain for most of her life, I have rarely heard her complain. She is a powerful prayer warrior, a positive example of a godly wife, and a wonderful neighbor to those who live around her. Whenever I talk to her, I always come away wanting to be like her. To me she is the epitome of an encouraging person. Every time I ask her how she is feeling, her response is always inspiring. "I'm very well," she cheerfully replies.

Along with a wonderful mother-in-law, I have others in my life who are constant sources of encouragement. I often jokingly say, "I don't need friends—I have sisters!" Of course I need my friends, but I do have three sisters who are always "on my side," ready to lift me up anytime I'm down. I'm even more blessed because I have great sisters who share the same bloodline, but I also have a group of women I meet with regularly who are sisters in Christ. Our little group of five, sometimes six, women has met every month for the past ten years. There's not a cynic in the bunch. We are free to candidly share our struggles, and many are the times when one of us has dumped her stress load on everyone's shoulders. We willingly help bear the load and turn to God for strength. By the time we leave each other's company, we're all feeling like we're being carried on the wings of everyone's prayers.

I realize that not everyone reading these pages has access to a "lunch bunch" like I do. But it doesn't take a group of friends to accomplish encouragement. One or two can be just as effective if—and this is an important if—they are uplifters and not down-draggers. I urge you to consider carefully who you spend time with. Are they encouragers or are they discouragers? You may need to make changes, such as discreetly avoiding the people who voice bleakness and actively pursuing those who are more positive. There are some people in our lives permanently, but at least you can limit your exposure to them and counteract their negativity by having plenty of optimistic people around.

Encourage Yourself

When we're feeling discouraged we often depend on other people to lift us up. And there is certainly nothing wrong with calling on a spouse, family member, or friend for support. Ecclesiastes 4:9-12 highlights this:

> Two are better than one because they have a good return for their labor. For if either of them falls, the one will lift up his companion. But woe to the one who falls when there is not another to lift him up. Furthermore, if two lie down together they keep warm, but how can one be warm alone? And if one can overpower him who is alone, two can resist him. A cord of three strands is not quickly torn apart.

Steve is my go-to person. He is usually upbeat, and he's my constant cheerleader and eager encourager. I'm so thankful to have him in my life. However, there are times when I must be ready and able and willing to encourage myself in the way David did. In 1 Samuel 30:6-8, we learn that he faced a terrible dilemma. While he and his men were conducting a military campaign, their enemy sacked Ziklag and took captive the soldiers' families. In their despair, the men blamed David and wanted to kill him. No doubt this was not only a very dangerous situation for him, it was also a very discouraging time. However, David did two things that helped him overcome the voice of discouragement. First, he "encouraged himself in the LORD his God" (verse 6). Next "David inquired of the LORD," asking what he should do (verse 8).

On occasion, when I would travel by myself to speak at women's events or Steve was soloing at men's events, one of us would remind the other as we parted ways, "Don't forget, the voice of the discourager will seem louder when you're alone. Don't let the solitude be his demolition grounds. Remember to do what David did!" We had both discovered that crying out for strength in prayer and staying before the Lord for wisdom are keys to quieting the voice of the discourager.

Another passage that speaks of encouraging ourselves is Judges 20:22: "The people, the men of Israel, encouraged themselves and arrayed for battle again in the place where they had arrayed themselves the first day. The sons of Israel went up and wept before the LORD until evening, and inquired of the Lord."

Do you see a pattern developing? Part of encouraging ourselves involves "inquiring of the Lord." Although the men of Israel had suffered terrible casualties, they did not allow themselves to be discouraged. They continued to fight and to ask God what they should do.

If you are battling the onslaught of the discourager, if his voice is in your ear at this time, I urge you to put this book down and encourage yourself. Remind yourself that you are one of "God's kids" and that you are not forgotten. Jesus said, "And surely I am with you always" (Matthew 28:20). And Psalm 55:22 tells us, "Cast your burden upon the Lord and He will sustain you." With these truths filling your heart, ask God what to do in the situation you are facing. Spend a few minutes doing this and then stop and listen for His reply. And follow His instructions! The next time the voice of discouragement returns, don't hesitate to repeat this process. Steve and I can testify to the effectiveness of this privilege God has given His own. We're still actively ministering through song and teaching, and we're sure this is what God has called us to do.

Be an Encourager

There is another proactive idea Steve and I find helpful when feeling discouraged, and we're confident it can work for you too. In a nutshell: Encourage someone who could use a lift. Even go out of your way to say something positive to someone. As Andy Griffith said to Opie in an episode of *Mayberry R.F.D.,* "Shoot for the good feeling!" Andy was encouraging Opie, who wasn't happy about having to do chores instead of playing with his friends. I say, "Amen, Brother Andy!" I've been on the receiving end of someone "shooting for the good feeling," and the act of kindness encouraged me to pass it on.

One such situation started at a drive-through window at a fast-food joint. I had ordered a hamburger and a senior coffee. When I pulled up to the window to pay my bill, the clerk told me the person in the car in front of me had paid for my order! I had no idea who this generous person was, and unfortunately, he or she was gone before I could see if I knew the occupant. I was left with a fist full of money, lunch, a grateful heart, and no one to thank. Whoever it was drove away with the smile that comes from doing something nice and thoughtful for someone else—whether a family member, friend, or stranger. And I drove away with a smile too.

• • • • •

It is nearly impossible to hear the voice of discouragement when you are busy encouraging someone.

• • • • •

A few days later I was shopping at our local Christian bookstore and found my own opportunity to shoot at the good feeling. I was standing in an aisle looking at the assorted books when I overheard a young man on his cell phone. He said, "I was wondering if I could pay you the money I owe you next week instead of this week. My pastor told me about a Bible I can buy that will be easier for me to understand." He went on to describe the translation and how he was anxious to get this version of God's Word so he could start reading it.

I made my selection from the books and proceeded to the counter to pay for my purchase. I asked the clerk if she could find out the cost of the Bible the young man mentioned and add it to my bill. She did as I requested, and I secretly showed her the young man who was to be the recipient of the Bible. She assured me she would take care of giving him the book. I left the store fully satisfied that I had encouraged someone and had provided healthy spiritual food at the same time!

The moral of my drive-through/bookstore report? It is nearly impossible to hear the voice of discouragement when you are busy encouraging someone. If you're feeling disheartened or depressed, find a way to be an encouragement to others. And what you do doesn't have to be a huge, life-changing event for the other person. Sometimes a good word or positive comment can provide enough smile to last an entire day or week. Here are a few "encouraging" ideas to help you get started.

• Babysit for a single mom so she can have some time to herself.

- Invite the children of a young couple over for the evening so the parents can have a date night.

- Invite a widow/widower for lunch (you can go to a restaurant or cook a meal at home). Give him or her an opportunity to share what's on his or her heart.

- Surprise your spouse by washing his or her vehicle.

- At the grocery store, offer to help someone by assisting with carrying out the groceries or loading the groceries into the person's car.

- Take a casserole or meal to a friend who isn't feeling well.

- Decide you're going to compliment three people as you go through your day…and then do it!

A "Heads Up" to Encouragers

As you seek ways to encourage others, be aware that the voice of discouragement will try to convince you to avoid doing such godly deeds. You might hear accusations that are meant to make you feel worthless and unusable so you won't take action and encourage people. If you hear that kind of nonsense, I hope you'll remember this email I received from a friend.

> The next time you feel like God can't use you, just remember…Noah was a drunk, Abraham was too old, Isaac was a daydreamer, Jacob was a liar, Leah was ugly, Joseph was abused, Moses had a stuttering problem, Gideon was afraid, Samson had long hair and was a womanizer, Rahab was a prostitute, Jeremiah and Timothy were too young, David had an affair and was a murderer, Elijah was suicidal, Isaiah preached naked, Jonah ran from God, Naomi was a widow, Job went bankrupt, John the Baptist ate bugs, Peter denied Christ, the disciples fell asleep while praying, Martha worried about everything, the Samaritan woman was divorced more than once, Zaccheus was very short, Paul was too religious, Timothy had an ulcer…and Lazarus was dead. What

do you have that's worse than these? So no more excuses! God can use you to your full potential. Besides you aren't the message, you are just the messenger.[1]

Silencing the voice of discouragement by being an encouragement to others will have a powerful effect on your world and beyond. This truth is well illustrated in a song Steve wrote. Almost every day this lyric goes through my mind. Why have these words impacted my life in such a way? Because I care about what others, especially my family, will remember about me when I'm gone. I want to be remembered as a positive, encouraging person.

Sweet on the Tongue

Old man Miller put up a good fight.
But word came this morning that he left us last night.
He had nearly nothing of this world's goods,
But there's one thing he could claim, we wish we all could

He had a good name. Just to say it tasted like honey.
You couldn't buy something like that 'cause there ain't
     enough money.
It's just how he lived until his days were done.
Lord, I want to have a name like his, sweet on the tongue.

It's better than silver; better than gold.
To leave no question marks in your story when it's told.
We went down to the church, and we all gathered in.
There was nothing but smiles all the while we talked
     about him.

'Cause he had a good name.
Just to say it tasted like honey.
You couldn't buy something like that 'cause there ain't
     enough money.
Lord, help me to live so when my days are done,
I'll have a name like his, sweet on the tongue.[2]

9

Embracing Only
What Is True

Listening to the condemning voices that come from our own hearts or the critical mouths of others can bring sheer misery to our souls. An important distinction to make is that the lasting damage that is often inflicted isn't necessarily caused by the actual words uttered. Rather, the pain is a result of our *choosing to believe* that the hurtful words are true. I was reminded of this reality not long ago while speaking to a distraught woman after one of our concerts.

The young lady told me that among all the things she had to do, she was also serving as the sole support and caretaker for her 75-year-old father. As she described their less-than-cheery relationship, it became apparent that he was a crotchety old bully who found pleasure in tormenting his daughter. His insensitivity and cruelty were matched by his apparent disrespect and unappreciative attitude toward the sacrifices his daughter was making on his behalf.

Although this lady's friends had encouraged her to leave her father and make him take care of himself, she felt sorry for him and wouldn't do that. She said, "There is no one to drive my dad to the doctor or fix his meals or make him take his medicine. He has no one in his life who is willing to take care of him. I am all he has."

Despite all the efforts she made to take care of her father, his critical attitude and harsh words were becoming more and more sadistic. She was finding it increasingly difficult to escape the verbal spears hurled at her. They were piercing her soul and shattering her sense of self-worth. With seemingly no regard for her feelings, he would level his vicious attacks and send her running from the room to bathe her bruised and wounded spirit in a bath of hot tears.

His unwarranted assaults included malicious comments along the lines of "You are so ignorant. No one would want to live with you. Look at you! You'll never amount to anything. You're good for nothing. You're lucky I let you live with me. No wonder your husband left you for that other woman."

Not only was her father biting the hand that was feeding him, he was also being used as a vocal weapon by the enemy of her soul to shoot gaping holes in her confidence. The tormentor—Satan—was using the one person in her life who should have been her cheerleader to rip her apart and destroy her. As I listened to her sad tale, it became obvious where the real problem lie. Wanting to give her a different perspective on her situation, I ventured into dangerous waters.

Looking directly into her eyes, I said, "You *are* a fat pig. I've never met anyone so morbidly obese. I can hardly see your eyes for all the layers of fat on your face. You must weigh a ton. How did you let yourself get this large?" As I uttered these hurtful words, I waited for her reaction. Just as I had expected, there was none. I said to her, "Why aren't you upset with me for saying these nasty things to you? Why aren't you crying your eyes out and running out of the room? Why aren't you arguing with me, telling me that I'm wrong to say those horrible things?"

She replied, "There's no need to argue because what you said is absurd. I'm not overweight. I've never had a problem with my size. The truth is I hardly weigh 100 pounds."

"Precisely," I said. "The words I said to you didn't wound you because you knew they were untrue. Only those things we accept as possible truth or truth can hurt us. So when your father begins tormenting you by calling you stupid and worthless, it hurts you because on some level and for some reason, you have chosen to agree with him. You've decided to believe the lies.

I saw the light of understanding come into the young woman's eyes.

I continued, "You can't make your father be nice and say sweet, encouraging things to you. However, what you *can do* is embrace what you know to be true and refuse to buy into or even entertain the deceptions of the enemy. When you cease to believe your father's hurtful criticism, his words will no longer have the power to hurt you."

• • • • •

To silence the voice of the tormentor, you
have to reject the lies of the enemy and
believe the truths found in God's Word.

• • • • •

With a thoughtful, hopeful look on her face, she asked me the question I was hoping she would.

"What is the truth I'm supposed to believe?"

Here was my chance to offer some lasting help for this young woman. "The truth is that you are precious and valuable in the sight of God. I encourage you to start reading and believing God's Word. The Bible has a lot to say on your identity. Jeremiah 29:11 says, "For I know the plans that I have for you," declares the LORD, "plans for welfare and not for calamity to give you a future and a hope."' Does this sound like your heavenly Father would be pleased about the terrible things your father has been saying to you? Do these words that show how much God loves you sound like He wants you to be tormented?"

"No, it doesn't," she replied.

"Doesn't it sound like God wants you to start believing He is on your side? I'm sorry but I think your father has been used as weapon by the hands of the enemy to hurt and undermine you. To silence the voice of the tormentor of your soul, you have to reject the lies of the enemy and believe the truths found in God's Word."

I went on to explain the importance of the divine duet in the quest to silence the tormentor. I quoted verses 12 and 13 of the Jeremiah 29 passage: "Then you will call upon Me and come and pray to Me, and I will listen to you. You will seek Me and find me when you search for Me with all your heart."

As God's glorious truths began to sink deep into her heart, I could see tears of relief forming. Slowly her anguished face gave way to a beautiful, peaceful smile. Much of her cold sadness was melted by the warmth of God's love and truth.

What had changed in the few minutes we talked? Her living situation certainly hadn't changed. She was going home to the same belligerent, pitiful father and the same thankless, difficult situation. Her assurance that she was not going home alone was the big change. With a determination to participate in the divine duet, she was taking home some spiritual weapons that would help her fend off the "lie arrows" and embrace the truth. The voice of the tormentor would be silenced at last.

I pray that her father will come to realize that his daughter is a lovely gift from God, someone who should be cherished and not abused. However, if he doesn't learn to appreciate her, there is one thing for sure: Her heavenly Father loves her dearly and is very proud of her.

The Antidote

Although the young lady I'd been talking to was determined to never again entertain the voice of the tormentor, before we parted ways I cautioned her to be on the alert for the enemy's continued onslaught. More than likely the devil would continue to try the various word barbs delivered through her dad. I promised to send her some additional weaponry she could use to deflect the devil's attacks and some effective antidotes for the poison that would be on any painful barbs that might reach her heart.

When I got home, I sent the following Scripture passages to the young woman, along with an encouraging note to refer to these verses anytime she sensed the unseen tormentor was attempting to hurt her again. And I know that when you hear any annoying and discouraging voices, they'll help you too. Why not write them down and put them where you can easily find them when you're having a hard time? Or better yet, why not memorize them so they'll always be in your mind and heart?

2 Corinthians 10:4: "The weapons of our warfare are not of the flesh, but divinely powerful for the destruction of fortresses."

1 John 4:4: "You are from God, little children, and have overcome them; because greater is He who is in you than he who is in the world." My paraphrase: "Greater is the One who lives in you than the one who comes against you."

2 Thessalonians 1:5-8 MSG: "All this trouble is a clear sign that God has decided to make you fit for the kingdom. You're suffering now, but justice is on the way. When the Master Jesus appears out of heaven in a blaze of fire with his strong angels, he'll even up the score by settling accounts with those who gave you such a bad time. His coming will be the break we've been waiting for. Those who refuse to know God and refuse to obey the Message will pay for what they've done. Eternal exile from the presence of the Master and his splendid power is their sentence. But on that very same day when He comes, He will be exalted by his followers and celebrated by all who believe—and all because you believed what we told you."

Matthew 11:28-30: "Come to Me, all who are weary and heavy-laden, and I will give you rest. Take My yoke upon you and learn from Me, for I am gentle and humble in heart, and you will find rest for your souls. For My yoke is easy and My burden is light."

Psalm 91: "He who dwells in the shelter of the Most High will abide in the shadow of the Almighty. I will say to the LORD, 'My refuge and my fortress, My God, in whom I trust!' For it is He who delivers you from the snare of the trapper and from the deadly pestilence. He will cover you with His pinions, and under His wings you may seek refuge; His faithfulness is a shield and bulwark.

"You will not be afraid of the terror by night, or of the arrow that flies by day; of the pestilence that stalks in darkness, or of the destruction that lays waste at noon. A thousand may fall at your side and ten thousand at your right hand, but it shall not approach you. You will only look on with your eyes and see the recompense of the wicked. For you have made the LORD, my refuge, even the Most High, your dwelling place. No evil will befall you, nor will any plague come near your tent.

"For He will give His angels charge concerning you, to guard you in all your ways. They will bear you up in their hands, that you do not strike your foot against a stone. You will tread upon the lion and cobra, the young lion and the serpent you will trample down. Because he has loved Me, therefore I will deliver him; I will set him securely on high, because he has known My name. He will call upon Me, and I will answer him; I will be with him in trouble; I will rescue him and honor him. With a long life I will satisfy him and let him see My salvation."

Psalm 42:11: "Why are you in despair, O my soul? And why have you become disturbed within me? Hope in God, for I shall yet praise Him, the help of my countenance and my God."

Here are more verses that will encourage you to turn to and put your trust in the Lord: Psalm 64:10; Proverbs 3:5-6; Jeremiah 9:23-24; Micah 6:8; John 3:16; 14:1; Romans 8:28-29; James 4:10.

An Important Note About Bullies

It took the woman whose father was so abusive with his tongue until adulthood to accept that it is only when we believe the slanderous lies of the enemy that those words will damage us. While I rejoice in her victory, I also think of how many children desperately need to learn what she has learned. Too many kids don't know that the bully's shouts are only effective when believed. And bullying isn't just a fad or stage kids go through. The outcome can be deadly. In one Texas town several girls bullied a girl so much she eventually committed suicide.

I am horrified by the evil people can inflict on other human beings. It seems like more and more kids are killing themselves because they believe their tormentors or they don't know how to silence the bullies.

Parents, I encourage you to counter the devastating messages your children might be hearing from bullies and other sources. Talk to them and teach them how to handle false statements and innuendoes about who they are and what they do.

Unfortunately, these negative forces most often strike their blows in schoolyards and classrooms. Here's how one wise mother handled her child's bully.

Teri, a mother of two, told me of a situation she encountered when her son was in the eighth grade. One of the popular kids at school took it upon himself to destroy Josh. The teen tyrant teased him and called him hurtful names that attacked his sexuality and the essence of who he was as a person. The verbal salvos and the emotional and physical assaults took a horrible toll on her son's spirit. Day after day, week after week, month after month the teasing continued. My friend was devastated as she watched her once studious son lose his desire to go to school. His heart suffered, his confidence suffered, his grades suffered.

As the bullying continued, Josh reacted exactly as the brute intended. His anguished screams of protest and his tears of anger made for entertaining drama for the instigator and the kids who witnessed the abuse. Josh became an even bigger target as other kids joined in to pick on him. Soon Josh's reactionary behavior got him in trouble with the teachers and administrators at the school.

What Josh couldn't see or understand was that once he was singled out for ridicule, the "gang" or "mob" mentality kicked into gear. His mom was torn about what to do. Josh didn't want to rat on the bully and believed that would make his situation even worse. When Teri shared with me what was going on, I drew on a childhood experience to offer advice.

On my family's dairy farm, we raised chickens along with our other critters. When a chicken gets injured, the wounded bird must be promptly removed from the rest of the flock because when the other fowl see the blood they begin to peck at it, further injuring the bird, sometimes to the point of killing it.

Teri realized even more that the bullying her son was going through was dangerous and that her son wasn't able to work it out on his own. The playing field was not level. The bully had the upper hand and was willing to do whatever it took to bring her child down. Against her son's protest she arranged a meeting with the principle.

As it turned out, the harasser's folks were powerful influences in the community and good friends and supporters of the principal. To add insult to injury, the boy was also the son of the school's guidance counselor. The close connection this malicious kid had with those in authority didn't deter Josh's mother. She demanded that action be taken against the bullying child. She was determined that nothing less than direct and effective steps needed to be taken to immediately put a stop to the unacceptable harassment of her son.

With respectful-but-firm persistence, Teri helped the principal recognize that if he didn't put a stop to the student's bad behavior, he and the school would be held legally accountable. It didn't take long after that for the guidance counselor to rein in her son. The torturing finally ceased.

Along with coming to her son's defense against the hurtful taunts of the bully, Teri also talked to Josh about how to defuse the power of such assaults. She made him aware that although school can be a vicious "chicken pen," there will usually be bullies around throughout his life. She talked with her son about how to deal with destructive messages and mean people. She shared who he should listen to and what he should and shouldn't believe. And by watching his mother's unyielding approach to the ordeal, Josh learned firsthand that quieting the voice of the bully can take effort and persistence, but it's a key to knowing and enjoying peace.

Another positive result of dealing effectively with a bully occurred that year. The young "felon in the making" had a change of heart as well as a change of destiny. He became a Christian and reported that he felt called to pursue ministry. While this outcome isn't guaranteed, if the bully had been allowed to continue tormenting Josh, his attitude and behavior might have further hardened his heart.

While Teri was being a caring and courageous mother, she might not have been aware that she was also presenting a good picture of our Father in heaven. He too comes alongside His children when the bully from hell wants to drag us to his awful place. May we all cling tightly to the hope found in Psalm 103:2,4: "Bless the LORD, O my soul, and forget none of His benefits…who redeems your life from the pit."

10

Countering Self-pity Through Praise

O f all the voices the enemy uses against us, perhaps the most destructive is the voice of self-pity. We know that the persistent voice of the accuser can leave us feeling dirty and mired down with guilt. The voice of shame calls us hurtful names, labeling us and killing our sense of worth. The scary voice of fear often challenges our trust and faith in God. The voice of discouragement can rob us of our joy and even our will to live. The malicious voice of the tormentor creates feelings of helplessness and hopelessness.

The damage done by the attacks of the enemy through the use of voices is severe. But the voice of self-pity is an insidious evil. Why is it so wicked? Because it uses our own voices to attack us, which makes it easier to believe the lies and leaves us feeling unloved and unappreciated.

In Hebrews 4:15 we are told that Jesus suffered every temptation we have or will ever endure. Does that mean that He has been tormented by the enemy's use of self-pity? Yes. I caught a glimpse of what that temptation might have looked like while watching the movie *The Passion of the Christ.*

Through the marvelous cinematography skills of Mel Gibson, who directed the epic story of Christ and His crucifixion, I was entranced by the scene that depicted Jesus praying in the Garden. In the movie Jesus fell on the ground and cried out to His Father. He was under such horrible stress that His face was covered with blood and sweat. Suddenly, from the shadows, a "being" emerged and began to talk to Him.

Using his most powerful weapon, the entity that represented Satan, in a cooing, commiserating, even tender voice, began calling into question the fairness of a God who would require His Son to suffer so terribly. He asked if Jesus thought it was right that one man should carry the burden of sin for the whole world. The enemy, in a hauntingly seductive voice went on to tell Jesus that the cost was too great. His words and voice were filled with pity as he used his "poor you" strategy of attack.

Charles Swindoll, in his book *The Greatest Life of All: Jesus,* says of that moment in Christ's struggle:

> Jesus wrestled with temptation. The terror of His coming ordeal gripped Him mercilessly. His blood dripped like sweat through the pores of His skin. As He stumbled through the darkness at Gethsemane, occasionally staggering and falling, thoughts kept returning to challenge His resolve. Why should He have to suffer on behalf of humanity? No moral imperative required God to sacrifice His Son. He would be no less holy or righteous if He allowed the race of sin-sick humans to suffer the just consequences of their own rebellion. Nothing compelled Jesus to complete the mission—nothing, that is, except love for a people He had made and obedience to His Father.[1]

Can't you hear the whispered voice of self-pity tap-tap-tapping away at Jesus' soul? Although Gibson and Swindoll's scenes are based on conjecture in their honest efforts to understand and share what Jesus endured that night so long ago in a garden far away, we do know that Satan was there. And he was up to his old tricks of tempting and testing.

We may not be privy to every detail said or done in the Garden of Gethsemane, but we do know that Jesus said to His Father in heaven, "Yet not My will, but Yours be done" (Luke 22:42). It was the devil's voice of self-pity that tried to stand between eternal salvation for the human race and the everlasting damnation of it. I'm so grateful Christ refused to listen to that voice! And you and I will have all of eternity to thank Him and praise Him for resisting it.

To Whom Will We Listen?

When we listen to the voice of self-pity, we give audience to the enemy of our souls. The end result is that we feel unloved and unappreciated. To be on guard so we can resist and reject the voice of self-pity, what can we do? Here are some suggestions of what that voice might sound like so we can readily identify the liar's attack methods. Have you ever heard the devil whisper these to you…using your own voice?

- I work very hard at my job, but it seems like I'm never the one who gets recognized. It's like I'm invisible until they have a task that no one else wants to do—then they remember my name. It's not right that I'm treated this way. I should quit. Then they'd know how much I do.

- The pastor thanked everyone who helped with Vacation Bible School—everyone but me, that is. Why did he leave me out? I helped as much as everyone else did. What do I have to do around here to get some recognition? I'm always the one treated like dirt. It's not fair.

- I can't count how many casseroles I've made through the years. I break my neck to help people, but do they ever give me anything in return? No. I didn't feel very well last week. Did anyone call and ask if they could bring me dinner? No again. I'm always the one giving and never the one receiving.

- I work my fingers to the bone trying to keep this house clean. Does anyone ever think to help me? No. I have a good mind to just stop doing anything around here. I should let them all starve to death. When I die, they're going to realize how much I did. That will show them.

- Every day I go to a job I hate. My wife and kids assume that I'm going to bring home a big paycheck, but they don't understand what I have to go through to get that money. And how do they help? They spend money like it's going out of style. I come home and the house is a wreck and no supper is on the table. The men I work with don't put up with that. Their families appreciate them, but not mine. Sometimes I'd like to leave in the morning and just not come home. Then they'd miss me—maybe.

- My kids never come to see me. I nearly died giving birth to them. Seriously, I had to have a blood transfusion even. Do you think they ever once thanked me for it? I never did lose the weight I gained when I was carrying them. I used to have a great figure, but I gave it up for them. I didn't have to be paid to go see my mother. They say they don't have the money for gasoline. Well, that doesn't keep them from going out to eat anytime they want to. I don't care how busy they are. I bet they go to see my daughter-in-law's parents all the time. I'm always the one left out. When my daughter called me this week, I gave her an earful. I told her just what I was thinking. She hung up on me. It's not right.

If any of these or similar statements have crossed your lips or played over and over in your mind, consider the likelihood that the enemy of your soul was speaking in your voice. That would be a disturbing thought if we didn't have Jesus with us and God's Word to help us defeat the devil's ploys!

A Warning About Self-pity

While we are all susceptible to the voice of self-pity, there is a group of people more at risk than others. Who are they? Those who live alone. I recognized the danger in aloneness the day I arrived at my dad's house a few weeks after my mother died.

Where once resided a bustling family of eight, he now sat quietly alone. I went to the back door and, as I walked in, I called his name. He was sitting in the den, and I could tell something was wrong immediately. He looked at me with bloodshot eyes. He'd been crying over the wasteland that he saw as his life. He choked, "Why didn't your mother marry me sooner? Why did she make us date for three years? We could have had more time together. I've been sitting here thinking maybe she didn't really love me."

• • • • •

God wants us to recall the many blessings He's given us.

• • • • •

The enemy had been warring against my poor old daddy. The voice of self-pity was in full assault mode. I was furious that Satan was picking on a lonely man who was so grief-stricken that he wasn't fighting back. I sat down, pulled out my "sword of the Spirit," and began to battle the devil. I shared with Dad passages that would help us silence the shouts of the enemy. We conversed about how much mom had always loved him and reminisced about how good God had been to them during their 52 years of marriage.

Then I shared a recording mom had made for me the previous Christmas. When she'd asked what I wanted for a present I mentioned wanting stories from her life. On the recording she expressed her immediate attraction to and enduring love for my dad from the minute she'd laid eyes on him. As he listened to her recorded voice, I could see his spirit lift. By the time we got up and left the den, Dad was smiling.

Reading God's Word and helping my dad remember many of the good things he'd enjoyed so far in his life reminded him of his many blessings and did much to burn away the fog of discouragement. God wants us to recall the many blessings He's given us. When we fail to do so, we create a void that the voice of self-pity has been waiting to fill.

When you sense the voice of self-pity whispering in your ear, read this section from Psalm 103 and the highlights from the other scriptures listed.

Psalm 103:1-5: "Bless the LORD, O my soul, and all that is within me, bless His holy name. Bless the LORD, O my soul, and forget none of His benefits; who pardons all your iniquities, who heals all your diseases; who redeems your life from the pit, who crowns you with lovingkindness and compassion; who satisfies your years with good things, so that your youth is renewed like the eagle."

Now, to cultivate a grateful heart that can quiet the voice of self-pity, take a closer look at the benefits and additional insights from these verses:

- *He has pardoned our sins.* "Pardon, and you will be pardoned" (Luke 6:37). "Be kind to one another, tender-hearted, forgiving each other, just as God in Christ also has forgiven you" (Ephesians 4:32). He doesn't need to give us anything more than this. Once He forgave our sins, everything else is gravy on our biscuit.

- *He has healed all our diseases.* Every stripe on His back was to make possible our healing (Isaiah 53:5). What a shame when we fail to go to Him when we have a physical need to be restored. He has already paid the price, and He wants us to ask for His help and healing so He didn't do it in vain. Remember, an unopened gift is a gift nonetheless.

- *He has redeemed our life from the pit.* Jesus came to give us life, and life more abundantly (John 10:10). His goodness is promised in this life as well as the next (Psalm 27:13).

- *He has crowned us with lovingkindness and compassion.* When we consider the love and mercy God has lavished on us, there is no room for complaining and self-indulgence (1 John 3:1).

- *He has filled our years with good things.* What good things has God given you? Family, job, home, church, friends, health, wealth, and prosperity? (Psalm 65:9-13). Have you praised Him for supplying "all your needs according to His riches in glory in Christ Jesus" (Philippians 4:19)?

As you remember God's blessings, why not say them aloud when you are alone with God? When you lift your voice of gratitude to God two amazing things will happen: The voice of self-pity will fade away and your focus will shift from self to the Savior.

Turn 3

"Draw near to God and
He will draw near to you."

11

Kissing the Chains

The nearness of God is my good.

Looking back over my life I can recall specific times when I've felt a particular closeness to the Lord. There have been delightful seasons of spiritual renewal that have drawn me closer to my heavenly Father. I've had the privilege of attending some awesome prayer retreats, I've sat under some inspiring Bible teaching, and I've experienced worship services that have helped me draw nearer to God in new and fresh ways. But the times that I have drawn the closest to the Lord and felt His undeniable presence, in what seemed like a concentrated form, have been those moments that were born out of my desperate need for His help and strength.

I felt God's presence and heard His voice of comfort reassuring me that He was going to take good care of my mother the night she abandoned her cancer-ridden body and moved into a glorified, heavenly one.

God's precious companionship kept me sane as I drove the eight-hour trip to West Virginia the day I received word that my daddy had died.

"Draw near to God and He will draw near to you" is a promise that encompasses all of our hopes for living victoriously in this life. Like the prodigal son's father who was waiting and watching for his boy to come home, our heavenly Father runs to meet us at our place of need. Our part in this divine duet is to scoot nearer and snuggle in toward our Father. God's part is to take us into His arms and hold us close.

Changing the Unacceptable; Accepting the Unchangeable

As God draws near to us in response to our reaching out to Him, He gives us the courage to change the situations that are unacceptable or unhealthy. He also gives us the strength to be victorious over the challenges we face that we can't change. Along with His strength, He gives us new perspectives to help us see how He can bring good out of dire circumstances. In fact, I have a reminder of this truth on my kitchen floor.

A few years ago we decided to take up the black-and-white NAS-CAR winner's circle-type tile in our kitchen and den area and replace it with hardwood. The system we chose was called a "floating floor." A truckload of cardboard boxes arrived, each box filled with 7 x 36-inch prefinished oak strips that were to be fitted and glued together. The workmen we hired to install it were highly skilled, and shortly after they unpacked their equipment they were well underway with the task. About an hour into their work I decided to step into the kitchen to check on the progress. That's when I saw it.

Near the sink, within the confines of one of the long sections of the flooring that had already been glued and toe-nailed down, was a small piece of hardwood about six inches by two inches long that was much lighter in color than the rest of that section, as well as the rest of the floor that was already in place around it. That small piece stood out like a light beam from a flashlight in a dark cave.

I interrupted the sweat-drenched workman who had moved well beyond that noticeable spot. "Excuse me, is that piece over there…" I pointed to the lighter-colored culprit, "going to stay? It doesn't seem to match the rest of the wood."

The poor fellow turned pale at the thought of having to take up the floor and start over. He tentatively said in his Tennessee drawl, "Well, ma'am, I'm just puttin' 'em down as they come out of the box. I reckon

I could take it all up and start over, but then we wouldn't have enough left to complete the job."

I sighed and searched for something to say. I came up with, "Okay, I suppose I can live with it."

Though it took some time to come to do that, today that small, off-colored, unalterable slice of oak in my floor is no longer a source of irritation. Instead, it has become valuable. I see it now as a constant reminder of how grateful I am for the rest of the house—including the nice hardwood floors.

In a similar way, life can yield some unchangeable situations or circumstances that can serve to draw us back to more valuable and eternal truths. Steve and I became acquainted with a young man who wrote to us after reading one of the outdoorsmen books my husband writes. The man is incarcerated in one of our country's prisons.

In his correspondence, he claims that his imprisonment is a horrible injustice. At the close of each letter, below his signature, he always adds, "Falsely accused, Wrongly convicted." My heart breaks each time I read those haunting words and wonder if they reflect the truth. With all appeals apparently exhausted, this young man seems to have no other choice but to draw near to God and allow God to come near to give Him strength to live each day accepting the unchangeable. My constant prayer for him is that he will come to see his circumstances as an "open door" to fulfilling God's plan for his life.

When I think of Steve's prison pen pal, I also consider the countless others who are crying out from all types of prisons, struggling to accept the circumstances they can't change and wondering how to find the peace of heart and mind they desperately need. When I imagine those cries my thoughts often go to a man in the Bible who can teach all of us how to look beyond the bars of circumstances to see the bigger picture.

The Apostle Paul—A Model Prisoner

Paul could have easily concluded his letters with the same proclamation of innocence as Steve's pen pal who is in prison. However, the apostle chose to see his imprisonment as an *opportunity to share Christ* with others. You might say that he chose to "kiss his chains" rather than to kick them.

If you read the book of Philippians without knowing the circumstances behind it, you might assume Paul was writing from a palace rather than a Roman prison. In this letter to the people in the church he established in Philippi, Paul shares openly and with full confidence that God is in the process of bringing good out of the difficulties he was facing. He writes of his imprisonment and the mistreatment he endured before and after his unlawful arrest: "Now I want you to know, brethren, that *my circumstances* have turned out for the greater progress of the gospel" (Philippians 1:12). Paul was indeed majoring on the main issue—spreading the message of Christ.

Joy in Spite of Circumstances

Although he didn't give specific details on his suffering in this letter, some of the circumstances Paul had to endure are listed in his letter to the people in the church in Corinth that he established. In 2 Corinthians 11 Paul writes that he:

- [participated] in far more labors
- [was] in far more imprisonments
- beaten times without number, often in danger of death
- five times…from the Jews thirty-nine lashes [40 lashes was considered deadly]
- three times…[was] beaten with rods
- once…[was] stoned
- three times…shipwrecked, a night and day…spent in the deep
- …[was] on frequent journeys
- in dangers from rivers
- dangers from robbers
- dangers from…countrymen
- dangers from the Gentiles

- dangers in the city
- dangers in the wilderness
- dangers on the sea
- dangers among false brethren
- been in labor and hardship
- through many sleepless nights
- in hunger and thirst
- in cold and exposure
- daily pressure of concern for believers and churches

When I read the long list of hardships Paul endured on behalf of his brothers and sisters in Christ, I wonder if I would be able to accept the difficulties with the same grace. I doubt I would have joyfully accepted the mistreatment Paul seems to have embraced. I feel a little panicked when I'm asked to sacrifice even a little bit, such as when our church called for a 24-hour fast.

So what will happen when the challenge is far greater? I know I'll turn to Paul's example and consider how he responded when he was required to give so much of himself. He found no satisfaction or purpose in recounting every slap, smack, whack, hit, spit, thump, or bump given to him for preaching and sharing Christ. He was willing to allow his circumstances to further his work so that in the end we would know that the chains didn't win—the victory was that God's will for his life was accomplished!

Preacher or Prisoner?

It goes against human wisdom to believe that the best way to launch a preaching career is from the confinement of a prison cell, but that's exactly what happened to the apostle Paul. After he arrived in Rome, Paul was placed in the 24/7 care of the Praetorian Guard. He was chained to one of these elite palace protectors constantly.[1] These Roman officers were assigned four-hour shifts to guard Paul.

Don't forget that Paul also didn't know if he would live to see the end of each day. And if he were sentenced to death, most likely his executioner would be one of the men who was bound to him daily.

• • • • •

Day after day, hour after hour, these men saw the gospel in action as Paul chose contentment over complaining, love over hatred, and peace over panic.

• • • • •

Envision yourself chained to someone whose job was to master the arts of inflicting pain, waging war, and conquering the weak. If that's not intimidating enough, imagine the coarseness of treatment and language that a man who is engaged in the killing profession might use. I'm pretty sure it wasn't the kind Paul was used to or preferred to encounter. Can you fathom the cultural, societal, physical, and religious differences between Paul, a former law-keeping Jewish Pharisee who had become a radical, grace-giving Christ follower, and a guard who was a pagan, emperor-worshipping, tough, gladiator-type killing machine? I imagine the devil was busy tempting Paul to act in retaliation or bitterness.

Most self-respecting Jewish men at that time in history would have been infuriated by the pagan, idol-worshipping Romans who had polluted God's holy city of Jerusalem, along with its religion and values, not to mention the violence they inflicted. The citizenry of Jerusalem were, for the most part, dominated and intimidated by the Roman troops. And the Romans also established laws and taxation the Jewish people had to follow and endure. These edicts were sources of humiliation and oppression for the Israelites of Palestine.

One decree that garnered extreme hatred between the Jews and Romans was the law that allowed the occupying Romans soldiers to demand that Jewish males carry their equipment for them. No matter what the Jewish person was doing, no matter what inconvenience it might cause, this law was punishable by death if the Jew didn't immediately comply with the request. In passive defiance of the law, it's said that Jewish fathers would take their sons out each morning and teach them how to calculate the exact measurement of a mile so that they wouldn't carry the Roman soldier's load one inch beyond the distance demanded by the law. A well-known instance of this law's use was put when Simon of Cyrene was commanded to carry Jesus' cross for him. Simon had no choice but to immediately do what the Roman soldiers told him.

Even with the poisonous history between the Jews and Romans, there is no indication in Scripture that Paul acted with resentment toward his captors. I believe he saw the guards not as his enemies but as *his* captives. Without being chained to Paul, how else would the emperor's elite bodyguards have heard the gospel of Christ? From the Scriptures we know that the guards allowed Paul to interact with them and have visitors. They heard Paul's prayerful petitions on their behalf. They listened to him dictate letters of instruction, correction, and salvation to the various believers and churches he was encouraging from afar.

No doubt the guards overheard Paul's conversations with the men of God who came to visit and encourage him. They listened as he explained the difference between the grace of God and the works of man. Day after day, hour after hour, these men saw the gospel in action as Paul chose contentment over complaining, love over hatred, and peace over panic. What do you think the guards thought when they heard Paul's teachings?

- "For to me, to live is Christ, and to die is gain" (Philippians 1:21).
- "Rejoice in the Lord always; again I will say, rejoice!" (4:4).
- "Be anxious for nothing, but in everything by prayer and supplication with thanksgiving let your request be made known to God" (4:6).
- "The peace of God, which surpasses all comprehension, will guard your hearts and your minds in Christ Jesus" (4:7).
- "I have learned to be content in whatever circumstances I am" (4:11).

- "I can do all things through [Christ] who strengthens me" (4:13).

Paul reported to the people in Philippi that the entire palace guard knew about Jesus (Philippians 1:13). No one knows exactly how many of the estimated 10,000 guards of Caesar were affected by Paul's captivity but some commentaries have estimated as many as 9000 of them heard the gospel. It seems that the guards who witnessed Paul's faith and testimony may have helped spread the message of Christ. What an amazing and encouraging commentary to know what can happen when one man is willing to kiss his chains rather than kick them.

Knowing the results of Paul's embracing his imprisonment encourages me to ask, "What kind of witness would I be if I were in a position similar to Paul's?" Would I have kissed my chains or kicked against them? I would like to say I would act in a loving and kind way toward the people involved. But if I felt cold, hard chains on my legs and wrists, it would be a supreme challenge to be nice to my captors. Even in my imagination I don't do well. If I were chained 24/7 to someone who was an owner/operator of an abortion clinic I'd probably spend a great deal of my time arguing, trying to convince him or her that abortion is really murdering babies, and that it is immoral and against God's principles. I can be feisty and persistent, so there's little doubt that I would make it clear that my captor needed to change his or her way.

Instead of winning people to the Lord, I'd probably make them even more antagonistic toward me and the issue. And this would mean I not only personally offended them, but I also probably made them more resistant to the message of Christ.

So knowing how I would react on my own, what do I do if I'm ever in that situation? Pay attention to Paul! Evidence shows that responding with contention and arguments is not how Paul acted toward his captors. Instead, he used his chains as an opportunity to share the love and forgiveness of Christ one-on-one with those tethered to him. It was not *in spite* of Paul's chains but *because of* them that the cause of Christ was advanced.

After two years, Paul was released from captivity. He was free for a short time, and then he was rearrested, beaten, and thrown into an underground dungeon to live out the remaining days of his life. At the decision of Nero, the insane emperor of Rome, Paul was beheaded for preaching the gospel. Paul continued to kiss his chains until the very end. During his final days he wrote:

> Do not be ashamed of the testimony of our Lord or of me His prisoner, but join with me in suffering for the gospel according to the power of God, who has saved us and called us with a holy calling, not according to our works, but according to His own purpose and grace which was granted us in Christ Jesus from all eternity, but now has been revealed by the appearing of our Savior Christ Jesus, who abolished death and brought life and immortality to light through the gospel, for which I was appointed a preacher and an apostle and a teacher. For this reason I also suffer these things, but I am not ashamed; for I know whom I have believed and I am convinced that He is able to guard what I have entrusted to Him until that day (2 Timothy 1:8-12).

Chain Kissers

I find it helpful and encouraging to consider a few examples of other Christians besides Paul who definitely chose to kiss their chains. I hope you will too. While looking at someone else's pain doesn't always help us when we are suffering, seeing how these people endured their circumstances might help us put our own chains in perspective.

John Bunyan

Born into poverty in 1628, John Bunyan had only two to four years of elementary schooling. His sparse education was just enough to prepare him to follow in his father's footsteps as a tinker (a mender of pots and kettles).

After losing his mother and two sisters to early deaths, John joined the army at age 16. After he returned from the war, he married Mary, who was also born in poverty. Within a few years Mary died, and John was left with four small children to raise, and one of them was blind. It was then that John turned to the Lord and submitted his life to Christ. He eventually began a lifelong practice of drawing near to God through prayer and study. God responded by drawing near to him. John began to preach the gospel of Jesus to all who would listen.

After the restoration of the monarchy in 1660, the law against unlicensed, nonconformist preaching was enforced. John's preaching was so popular and powerful and unacceptable to leaders in the Church of England that he was thrown into jail. Although sentenced to three months, John refused to promise that he would quit preaching. He said, "If you release me today, I will preach tomorrow." As a result of that determination to share the love and salvation through Christ, he was incarcerated for 12 years! Many people interceded on his behalf, including his wife, Elizabeth, but to no avail.[2]

John saw his imprisonment as an opportunity to minister to those in prison with him. Each day he preached in the jail courtyard. He had a large audience of prisoners, and hundreds of the citizens of the town of Bedford and surrounding area would also come to the prison daily to hear him. They would stand outside the fence to listen to him share the "Bread of Life" found in the Scriptures.

After being released in 1672, John preached for three more years. He was then rearrested for preaching in an unsanctioned church. This time he wasn't allowed to preach in the courtyard. He was placed in a cell deep within the bowels of the prison. The prison officials who wanted to silence him didn't succeed. Through his solitude he spoke his loudest sermon! During that time of isolation, John Bunyan wrote the mighty book *The Pilgrim's Progress*. This great Christian classic has ministered the gospel of Jesus to tens of millions throughout the world. Many believe this book is the most widely read and translated book in the world after the Bible.

Like the apostle Paul, John Bunyan learned that the chains of his imprisonment were not obstacles but opportunities to do what he could not do otherwise. His kissing the chains reminds us that living our lives free from grumbling and complaining about our circumstances can give us unique ways to live life filled with joy and purpose even when bad things happen.

Fanny Crosby

When Fanny Crosby was six weeks old, she caught a cold and contracted an eye infection. With the family physician unavailable, her parents followed the advice of the doctor who was sent in his place. This unskilled doctor recommended they treat the eye infection by placing hot poultices on her inflamed eyelids. The infection cleared up, but scars formed on her eyes, and Fanny became permanently blind. A few months later, Fanny's father grew ill and died. Her mother, Mercy Crosby, widowed at 21, hired out as a maid while her Grandmother Eunice took care of Fanny.

A landlady of the Crosbys also played an important role in Fanny's development. Fanny memorized the Bible, sometimes learning five chapters a week! She knew the first five books of the Bible by memory along with the four Gospels, Proverbs, and many of the psalms.

Her blindness, Fanny believed, forced her to develop her memory and her powers of concentration more than others. She didn't look at her blindness as a terrible tragedy. Even at eight years old she composed this unforgettable lyric.

Oh, what a happy child I am,
Although I cannot see!
I am resolved that in this world
Contented I will be!
How many blessings I enjoy
That other people don't!
So weep or sigh because I'm blind
I cannot—nor I won't.

Fanny was a beautiful example of one who, as a result of drawing near to God and Him drawing near to her, was able to see the value of her chains of blindness. As an adult she said, "It was the best thing that could have happened to me. How in the world could I have lived such a helpful life as I have lived had I not been blind?"

And just what did she do that was so helpful? She is known as one of the most prolific hymn writers in history, having more than 8000 songs credited to her. Since some publishers were hesitant to have so many hymns by one person in their music books, Fanny used close to 100 pseudonyms. She penned such beloved hymns as "Blessed Assurance," "Jesus Is Tenderly Calling You Home," and "To God Be the Glory."

Undeniably, our world is a better place because Fanny Crosby decided to take the "lemons of her life and make sweet lemonade."

Joni Eareckson Tada

A great example of someone who has not let disability keep her from fulfilling God's wonderful plan is Joni Eareckson Tada. Due to a diving accident at age 17, Joni has been a quadriplegic and confined to a wheelchair for more than four decades. Her struggle with her "chains" is chronicled in her bestselling book *Joni*.

During two years of rehabilitation, Joni spent long months learning how to paint holding the brush between her teeth. Her beautiful creations are in demand by collectors of fine art. She's authored more than 35 books, traveled to more than 45 countries, and received numerous awards and honorary doctoral degrees. Joni has redefined disabled and inspired others who have been impaired physically to succeed. God has proven through His presence in her life that there is no circumstance (no matter how terrible), no accident (no matter how tragic) that can separate her from His love and His plans.

Joni is founder and president of Joni and Friends, an organization accelerating Christian outreach in the disability community. Many years ago our family was privileged to minister alongside Joni during a weekend event. My children were smitten by her beautiful demeanor and gentle spirit. My daughter, Heidi, wasn't quite ten at the time and was so impressed by Joni's delightful personality that she innocently announced, "When I grow up, I want to be in a wheelchair." Could there be any greater compliment my daughter could have paid Joni?

Some time later we were with Joni once again at an event. I told her what Heidi had said about wanting to be in a wheelchair just like her. She responded with a lovely laugh and called Heidi to her side. She tenderly said, "Dear child, I would never want you to have to be in a wheelchair. But I thank you for such a sweet thought."

Heidi was responding to the "salt effect" of one who has chosen to view her wheelchair as a platform to make a difference in her world. Joni is living proof that we can all look beyond our circumstances and see countless opportunities before us for living for Christ and sharing His love.

Today Joni continues to inspire people as she battles breast cancer. It's not surprising that she and her husband, Ken, are looking to God for wisdom and perseverance. Joni wrote in her blog, "Rest assured that Ken and I are utterly convinced that God is going to use this to stretch our faith, brighten our hope, and strengthen our witness."[3]

Nick Vujicic

While Joni has been able to use her mind and paralyzed limbs to reach out to the able and the disabled, Nick Vujicic has reached millions of people without any limbs at all. His ministry, Life Without Limbs, is a beautiful example of yet another chain kisser who has changed the world by seeing his disability as an opportunity not an obstacle.

Born without arms or legs, Nick has traveled the world teaching all who would listen to him that we are only limited when we choose to be. Hearing Jeremiah 29:11 spoken from the heart of this man is life-changing! He's chosen to look at life through the "context lenses" of the goodness of God. To watch him on film looking across an audience of "normal" limbed folks and share that verse is awe-inspiring: "'For I know the plans I have for you,' says the LORD. 'They are plans for good and not for disaster, to give you a future and a hope.'" I can't help but be moved to tears. From no limbs to no limits, Nick's smiling face and infectious zeal for life reaches out and touches the hearts of all who hear him.

Our Suffering Is Never Squandered

The apostle Paul, John Bunyan, Fanny Crosby, Joni Eareckson Tada, and Nick Vujicic could say with Job of old, "I know that You can do all things, and that no purpose of Yours can be thwarted" (Job 42:2). With the nearness of God being their source of strength and protection, these individuals knew that nothing could touch them that doesn't pass through the loving filter of God's hand. Their stories can remind us that when pain and sorrow touch us, we can count on the comforting fact that God will make sure that our suffering is not squandered. Our God is not a wasteful God! John 6:12 says, "When they had all had enough to eat, [Jesus] said to his disciples, 'Gather the pieces that are left over. Let nothing be wasted'" (NIV.)

If God is careful to not waste even the bits of leftover bread and fish then be assured that He will not allow the difficulties of our lives to be wasted. This truth is expressed in yet another way through the familiar and comforting words of Romans 8:28. As you read this verse, may God come near to you even now as you feel the chains that remind you of your need for His presence: "We know that God causes all things to work together for good to those who love God, to those who are called according to His purpose."

Easier Said Than Done

Abraham Lincoln was walking down the street with his two sons, who were crying and fighting. "What's the matter with the boys?" a friend asked. "The same thing that's wrong with the whole world," Lincoln replied. "I have three walnuts and each of the boys wants two!"[4]

One of the hazards of suggesting that a person consider "kissing his or her chains" instead of fighting against them is that you run the risk of sounding cold and unfeeling about someone else's pain. It's a little like saying to someone, "I hear you're having minor surgery," when surgery is only *minor* if someone else is having it. When you're the one who is hurting, for whatever reason and to whatever degree, it doesn't feel like *minor* pain. Even though this may seem obvious, I learned this lesson the hard way. I was guilty of offering a "word not fitly spoken for the moment."

One night long ago Steve and I were at church enjoying the fellow-ship at an early-October, mid-week prayer meeting, not knowing that our vehicle was being vandalized. The thief broke the driver's side window and stole Steve's vintage Gibson acoustic guitar. At the time we didn't have the money to fix the window, and the guitar was one Steve had owned and loved for many years. Plus it was his only guitar, and since playing music was our livelihood, the bandit hit us hard.

When we discovered the crime, we stood in the parking lot in shock. People gathered around to see and talk about what had happened. Some dear friends saw the commotion and walked over to check things out. We explained we had been the victims of a burglary. Without hesitating they cheerfully offered words that were supposed to encourage us, but they felt more like a knife going through our aching hearts: "Now you two need to just praise the Lord! Come on. In everything we are to praise Him and give Him glory. You need to thank the Lord that your guitar has been stolen. There's a reason for it, and you'll find it out later."

There was nothing wrong with the words they said. And we are to offer praise in everything. But their words and attitude were given at the wrong time. I shot back, "When it's *your* guitar, *you* can rejoice. Right now I don't feel like praising God. I'm upset and angry at the creep who did this."

Through the years there have been many opportunities for me to encourage others who have suddenly found themselves in dismal situations. Nearly every time it has happened, I've thought about that fateful night when our guitar was stolen and how I felt when I heard our friends' ill-timed admonishment. This helps me remember how the people are probably feeling so I can respond more sensitively.

Thankfully our situation had a happy ending. Later on that same evening the stolen guitar was discovered in the alley leading from the church to the street. The thief had been surprised by a man driving down that little road after church. The car lights made the crook panic, and he threw the guitar into the weeds and ran away. The man in the car stopped, got out of his vehicle, and retrieved the guitar. When he opened the case he found our name and address inside. He returned the Gibson, and Steve still plays it today.

Through this situation I've concluded that a more appropriate and uplifting encouragement in times of trouble would be more in line with the sentiments found in Romans 12:15: "Rejoice with those who rejoice, and weep with those who weep." Or as the Message Bible puts it, "Laugh with your happy friends when they're happy; share tears when they're down."

It is with that attitude of compassion that I want to continue with this matter of "kissing the chains." Please know that my goal for going down this road with you is to help you get through this difficult time in your life.

Chain Kissers

If you go to the aisles of most hardware stores where the chains are displayed, you'll discover that they come in varying grades. They range from smooth, lightweight plastic to thick metal types. In the same way, there are varying grades of chains that people deal with on spiritual, physical, and emotional levels. Some are easily broken with minimal effort, such as a slight shift in attitude or a doctor's prescription for hormone-replacement therapy. Some, however, bear chains that are heavy and abrasive. In the next chapter we'll look at some of the heavier chains that can bind the soul, the spirit, and the body and how to break them.

Living Vibrantly, Chains and All

The source of pain is as varied as there are people who experience it. At a woman's conference on what binds us and keeps us feeling emotionally and spiritually exhausted, I asked the participants to write down what they considered chains in their lives. Here are a few of their responses.

- I'm single and wish I had a family of my own.
- I've gotten our family into deep debt using credit cards.
- I am angry all the time.
- I hate to admit that I am a jealous person.
- I feel very insecure.
- My weight holds me back from loving myself.
- I have cancer in my body.
- My mother-in-law lives with us.
- I battle depression all the time.
- I am addicted to pornography.
- My job situation is terrible. It's a tough place to be a Christian.
- I feel suffocated by my kids. There seems to be no end to their demands.

- I live with a critical, bi-polar, mean husband who never has a kind word to say to me.

- I'm still dealing with the pain of being molested by my stepfather.

- I have terrible guilt from the way I've lived my life in the past.

- I struggle with the shame of being raped.

- I'm in a marriage that looks nothing like what we had years ago.

- I am so lonely. I don't have any friends.

- My son has destroyed his marriage, and my grandchildren are in the middle of it all.

- My daughter engages in behaviors that will destroy her life. I feel helpless.

- I feel the pressure of financial problems. We have to pay for college, and we're already up to our ears in credit card debt.

- My ex-husband is still a problem for me.

- I struggle with masturbation. I'm filled with self-loathing.

- I am held captive by my judgmental attitude toward others. I always see the negative side of things.

- I am paralyzed by fear of what might happen.

- I am filled with self-doubt.

- My children neglect me. I feel unloved.

- I am always sick. I hate being so physically weak.

- Menopause feels like a cage—a hot cage…no, a cold cage.

As I read through the responses, I was reminded of an old saying: "If everyone were to hang their problems on a clothesline for the world to see, at the end of the day we would probably take our own problems back into the house."

Most of us have some kind of burden or fetters on our lives. Whether they're large or small, the primary decision we need to make is whether we'll "kiss the chains" like Paul did or kick and struggle against them.

If there is to be some level of peace and joy in our hearts, the kind that spiritually sustains us and blesses those around us, the obvious answer is that we need to choose to kiss the chains. Though accepting the tethers is the right thing to do, how can we possibly do it? It's counter to our humanness to look for the good in discomfort and pain. We can only be successful when we take our eyes off the chains and look for the divine purpose that can come about through it.

There are those who look, but not everyone sees. Some have sight, others have insight. To help you develop peace-yielding insight, let's untangle a few of the more common chains we encounter. Obviously we can't cover them all, so we'll take a close look at a few examples mentioned at that women's conference and the possible good that might be found in them. Hopefully this will help you see more clearly the purpose of the chains affecting your life right now.

Chained to a Job

"My job situation is terrible. It's a tough place to be a Christian." Being a Christian in a work environment that isn't friendly to your faith can be one of the most challenging and bleak situations we deal with on a social level. This is true because a job is so daily. With that kind of grind facing us regularly, it's easy to take our eyes off of the divine purpose of being at that job and start looking at it as nothing more than a paycheck-yielding ball and chain.

Can you relate to this chain? Do you go to work each day feeling unappreciated by a boss who is unjust and demanding? Are you locked into employment that leaves you bored and feeling unaccomplished? Have you had people outside your situation offer pat answers, such as, "If you don't like your job, just quit and find another one." In these days of economic uncertainty, unemployment, and underemployment, it's not always a wise decision to leave a job that is secure and profitable just because you're not thrilled by it.

Now if you are expected to compromise your moral, ethical, legal, or personal honor, that's a different story. Then the issue shifts dramatically from income to integrity. Years ago, when I was fresh out of college, I was offered a job in a small Christian bookstore. I was the only employee, and the responsibility for the daily operation of the store fell on my shoulders. Since I was in desperate need of the job, I was willing to do almost anything the owner asked of me.

A few days into the training, I was informed that two sets of accounting books were to be kept. One was for tax purposes; the other was to record the actual transactions for the day's receipts. I was appalled that a Christian-based store would operate in such a way. Being overworked and underpaid was something I was willing to endure, but being party to illegal and morally reprehensible actions was not an option. If this scenario sounds similar to yours, it may well be time to step away for legal and moral reasons.

If your job situation doesn't threaten your standards but fiercely challenges your attitudes about life and your Christian walk, you can choose to stay. If you do that, you have two options: Kick the job chain or kiss it.

How can you evaluate how well you're kissing...or if you're really kicking?

- Do your fellow employees hear you grumbling and complaining about the work conditions, your pay, or your work assignments?
- Do you join in the gossip mill with co-workers?
- Are you making comments about people you wouldn't say to them?
- Do you make racial, ethnic, religious, or political comments that are unkind, untrue, or unnecessary?
- Do you exclude fellow workers by engaging in a clique mentality?
- Do you take longer breaks than permitted?
- Does your lunch time last longer than allowed?
- Do you play games on your work computer instead of working?
- Do you send personal emails or browse the Internet—spending work time on nonwork-related activities?

If the answer to any of these questions is yes, you could be kicking the chains. If your answer is yes to several of them or more, you *are* kicking the chains. If you are kicking the chains, lift your heart to God and ask Him to help you discover His purpose for your presence at that job. Seek opportunities you might have overlooked that God can use you in. You won't be able to kiss the chains until you do find a worthwhile purpose. The good news is that God's Word gives you a great starting place! Psalm 4:6-8 is very insightful:

> Many are saying, "Who will show us any good?"
> Lift up the light of Your countenance upon us,
>   O LORD!
> You have put gladness in my heart, more than
>   when their grain and new wine abound.
> In peace I will both lie down and sleep, for You alone,
>   O LORD, make me to dwell in safety.

The word "show" in the first line of this passage is very important. This word is akin to the concept of "video." Imagine God's light shining through you to produce a movie people can watch. Hopefully you will project God's goodness and love so the people around you will be drawn to Him.

• • • • •

**Does your behavior and attitude on
the job reflect well on Christ?**

• • • • •

Not long ago I received an email with a quip I enjoyed: "A lighthouse doesn't blow its horn, it just stands and shines." I love this! A lot of truth is packed in those few words. Think about being a lighthouse at work. Granted, there are job-related situations where you may be restricted in what you can share about your faith. Perhaps your workplace is one that stifles your desire to reveal your heartfelt beliefs in Jesus Christ. As part of kissing your chains, work within the limits your employer sets. However, no one can keep you from reflecting God's life-changing light of love shining through you. No one can keep you from being kind and compassionate. No one can keep you from silently and unobtrusively praying for co-workers. No one can keep you from offering words of affirmation. The darker the night, the brighter the light shines. Be God's light shining bright and let Him draw people to you outside of your work environment where you might have opportunities to share your faith and offer encouragement and insights.

If you're chained to a job you don't particularly like and yet choose to stay in, I encourage you to ask God how you can use your position for a greater cause instead of just a paycheck. When people notice how you're different, they'll want to talk to you about it. Then you can extend invitations to your fellow employees (or even your boss) to go to your church or attend events where the gospel of Jesus Christ will be shared.

The caveat is that you need to be living your faith and being a great representative for Jesus. Does your behavior and attitude on the job reflect well on Christ? If you haven't been living as Christ called you to live, consider an insightful comment attributed to Alexander the Great, the king of Macedonia and conqueror of the extensive Persian Empire (circa 300 BC). During his reign it was common for mothers to name their children after the ruler. A lad committed a crime and was brought before Alexander the Great. The king asked the boy what his name was. The man replied, "My name is Alexander." The young king commanded, "Change your name or change your ways!"

Is God saying the same thing to you? If you know your behavior at your job has been less than stellar, work on upgrading the impression you've made in the minds of those you work with. When you've accomplished that worthy task, invite them to your home and church with full assurance they won't scoff at Christianity.

Making your chief intent to bring good to the name of Christ is a noble goal, especially in the workplace. By adorning your name with honorable behavior on your job you can do just that. Plus this will help you lift your eyes off the chains and put them on something of far greater value—the reward of God's favor on your life. The third chapter of Paul's letter to the Colossians says, "Whatever you do, do your work heartily, as for the Lord rather than for men, knowing that from the Lord you will receive the reward of the inheritance. It is the Lord Christ whom you serve" (verses 23-24).

Chained to Your Home

"I feel suffocated by my kids. There seems to be no end to their demands." Children add a lot of stress to life. Even though the blessings outweigh the negatives, sometimes it doesn't seem that way. I remember what my mother said one day while in the throes of raising six of us. We were typical kids who fought and argued about everything. One day when we were acting non-angelic, mom shouted for us all to stop and be quiet. Momentarily we halted our assaults and insults. When mom realized she had our attention, she seized this rare moment to say something that still hangs in the air where that house once stood: "I want each one of you to know that not a'one of you was planned." Can't you just hear the frustration in my mother's comment?

The irritations that my mother, and mothers like her throughout the ages, have suffered should not be dismissed lightly. No doubt, one of the most grueling jobs on the face of this earth is being a mother to children who live at home. Looking at the job of parenting in its larger context will assist us in our willingness to "kiss these chains" rather than kick them.

Years ago when I was in the middle of the rigors of mothering two at-home kids, I heard someone say, "The job of being a parent is a lot like being an architect. An architect is one who builds dwelling places. In essence, as parents, we are building temples of flesh where God wants to live."

When I placed my role as a parent in the framework of an "architect of the heart," it helped me be even more determined to do it well. Granted, it is not always easy to maintain that viewpoint. I was reminded of this one day when Heidi called to share that she was having a particularly challenging day with her young daughter. She told me she was afraid Lily had experienced a seizure.

Her use of the word "seizure" immediately got my full attention. Concerned, I asked her to describe what had happened. Heidi said she asked Lily to put her toys away so she could take her nap. Suddenly Lily fell on the floor, started kicking wildly, and her face turned purple. As I listened to Heidi, I quickly relaxed. "Heidi," I quietly said, "that's not a seizure; that's a fit—a temper tantrum."

Heidi's voice was filled with the fatigue and frustration that a mom feels when she's being severely tested beyond her ability to cope. She said, "Why didn't you tell me it would be this hard?"

I replied, "Heidi, I didn't tell you it would be easy either. I only said it would be worth it."

When my children were little, I was totally consumed with all the work it takes to keep our home running smoothly. Looking back, I know I missed out on a lot of good memory-making opportunities. There were times when I chose to straighten up the house when I could have been working a puzzle with one of the kids. There were times when I swept the floor when I could have been rolling on it with them. I encourage you to spend as much time with your kids as you can. You'll be surprised at how fast they grow up!

That reality was made clear to me by the untimely death of a dear friend and young mother Steve and I knew in Texas. Donna had been sick only a short time, and her death was a shock. Her passing left her husband, Jim, with a shattered heart and two little boys and an infant daughter without a mother's love and comfort. As fall arrived that year, my heart was burdened for the family's loss of such a dear wife and mother. One day when I went down to our laundry room in the basement, I was folding yet another load of clothes when my thoughts drifted to Donna. My mind was soon brought back to the present by the sights and sounds of Steve and the kids playing in the leaf pile in the backyard.

As I looked out the small window, I heard peals of laughter and screams of delight as the three of them tossed leaves into the air and chased one another around the yard. My first response to this beautiful sight of family in the midst of play wasn't what you might expect. I didn't look at the smiles that spread across their sweet and serene faces. I didn't listen to the sounds of laughter coming from sheer enjoyment as a melodious moment. No, I thought about all the leaves that weren't being raked and bagged as I had requested. I thought about the grass stains that would be marring the new sneakers we'd just bought for the kids. I thought about the dirt on their blue jeans that would add to my laundry burden. I thought about the baths that would have to be taken and the hair that would have to be washed because of this time of fun.

Immediately after thinking these selfish thoughts, I was ashamed. I wasn't considering the beautiful memories that were being written on our kids' hearts as they played with their dad. I wasn't looking at the big picture filled with joy because I was blinded by the present. Then I thought of Donna again. I wondered what she would be saying in that instant if she were standing next to me: "Don't you think it would be a good idea to let the laundry wait for a while and go out there and play with your husband and those kids? If it were me, you'd better believe that's what I would be doing."

Shaken by the quiet whisper of insight that my behavior and attitude weren't on the right track, I dropped the laundry I was folding back into the basket, grabbed my coat and gloves, and hurried outside to frolic with my family. That day I made the best decision! I consciously embraced the chains of home and found joy in the midst of the work.

I wish I could tell you I always made good decisions when it came to spending time with my family from that time on. But my tendency to be a workaholic and perfectionist has made this a challenge. At my core I'm more of a "Martha" person than a "Mary" (see Luke 10). But as I learned to kiss my chains, the decision and ability to lighten up did get easier.

In 1 Timothy 2:15, we are reminded that "women will be preserved through the bearing of children if they continue in faith and love and sanctify with self-restraint." For the longest time I wondered what this passage meant. While commentaries offer a variety of opinions, I've concluded that when you become a parent, you have to make a concerted effort to be unselfish. You have to put the needs of your children above your own because these little beings are totally dependent on you. And if you choose to not acknowledge this reality, your sight will be limited to only seeing the chains (sacrifices) and not the opportunities (blessings) God is giving you as one of His architects.

And yes, if you're waiting for your kids to say thank you for working on your attitude, don't hold your breath. Your kids are most concerned with *their* happiness. Unselfishness is something that is taught, nurtured, and developed. Someday they'll rise up and call you blessed, but for now your kids are only going to rise up and ask, "What's for breakfast?" When they do, pucker up. It's time to do some chain kissing.

Chained to Suffering

"I have cancer in my body." Illness and suffering are chains that are very difficult to kiss. For people whose bodies have seemingly turned against them and become their worst enemies, the temptation to despair is ever present. Often they wonder how they're supposed to respond to the stress and restrictions that illnesses and diseases bring.

From time to time I have dealt with severe back pain. I have a nerve that every once in a while gets pinched, which takes me off my feet. I've had episodes when I am in such terrible pain that it seems like the joy and peace of the Lord are soaked up by the sponge of depression. When my back suddenly "goes out," I often can't sit, lie down, or walk in any kind of comfort. While these times aren't fun, I am well aware that my "back chain" is nothing compared to what some folks face when it comes to pain and disease.

I watched as my mother struggled to embrace her physical suffering as she battled cancer for 10 years. And believe me, she was not one to go down without a fight. I have yet to meet anyone with more spirit and spunk than Mom. Yet when she was diagnosed with non-Hodgkin's lymphoma at the age of 64, she was faced with a foe greater than anything she'd ever encountered. She was in the battle of a lifetime.

Mom was very good about going to the doctor and having her annual check-ups. She didn't drink alcohol of any kind or use any form of tobacco. She lived a life free from drugs—legal and illegal. She and dad drank well water, grew their own vegetables, and butchered their own meat. She lived in the country with its abundance of fresh air and healthy activities. Since she had always made good decisions about her health, she considered cancer something she didn't deserve.

In the beginning of 1986, Mom was losing weight so she went to the doctor. The doctor's caviler attitude was reflected in his response: "Good. You need to lose weight. You're too heavy." Mom's reply should have alerted the doctor. She said, "I'm not on a diet. Why would I be losing weight?" He didn't listen to her. This went on for many months. Finally, in the fall of that year, the family went with her to her appointment. This time the doctor ran the tests that should have been done months earlier. Mom had cancer, and it was very advanced. It had reached the incurable stage.

When the diagnosis was first made, Mom was given only a few months to live. However, as she responded to the chemo treatments, her prognosis was revised.

The shock, disappointment, and anger over the way her doctor had let her down was monumental. Mom, infuriated, had no intention of forgiving the doctor for his negligence. And living with the threat of imminent death and uncertainty regarding her life on earth, the days she had left were tainted with an edge of dread. During the 10 years she lived after her diagnosis, she was able to see many of her grandchildren born and experienced many delightful occasions. However, the happy times were overshadowed by her inability or unwillingness to kiss her chains. The anger and fear that accompanied her disease robbed her of many enjoyable moments.

Although Mom had a hard time living with cancer, when the last days came, she faced them with the same courage we had come to expect from her. She had one bit of unfinished business though. Her anger toward the doctor who had let her down had never been put to rest. In God's grace and mercy, when Mom was admitted to the hospital for the last time, can you guess who the admitting doctor was in the emergency room? That's right! Mom's former doctor was the one who attended to her.

As he looked at what cancer had done to a once strong, beautiful woman, he was moved with sorrow and regret. He said, "Mrs. Williamson, I'm so sorry for what has happened to you." When Mother responded to his sincere apology with a tender and humble concession that in her own way was a statement of full forgiveness, I knew she had at last kissed the chains of her sickness. She simply replied, "We all make mistakes. It's all right."

Oh, friend, it is never too late to kiss the chains. No matter how hard it is to accept the instruments of suffering, kicking those terrible chains only robs us of precious time that we don't have to waste. In the midst of the suffering, reach out to others and offer them comfort. Find opportunities within your situation to serve and reflect Christ's compassion.

Chained to Loneliness

"I am so lonely. I don't have any friends." When my mom died, she left a grieving husband she'd been married to for more than 52 years. Dad was terribly lonely. I'll never forget the pitiful sound of his voice when he said, "Loneliness hurts worse than cancer." If anyone knew the comparison between the two, he did because he had experienced the pain of both. The following lyric was written by Steve a few months after my mother died. It describes my dad's life as a widower.

The Man in Aisle Two

Dear friend of mine, I write you this letter,
How have you been since your mother passed away?
No one 'round here will ever forget her,
And I need to tell you what I saw today.
I saw your dad at the grocery this morning.
He was wandering, lost, down aisle number two.
We talked for a while. I said, "How've you been doing?"
He said he was fine, but in his arms he held the truth.

He had one TV dinner and a box of saltines,
One shiny red apple and a can of beans,
One small jar of coffee, the kind you make with a spoon.
Dear friend of mine, are you coming home soon?

How quick he said yes when I invited him over.
And he smiled when I said, "Suppertime,
we'll set a place for three."
As I was leaving, I looked over my shoulder,
And I wondered how you'd feel if you could see...

That he had one TV dinner and a box of saltines,
One shiny red apple and a can of beans,
One small jar of coffee, the kind you make with a spoon.
Dear friend of mine, are you coming home soon?[1]

Embodied in this lyric is one of the answers my dad found to overcoming the lonely feelings. He found that being willing to embrace the efforts of those who reached out to him was a key way to unlock the chains of loneliness. As he began to accept invitations for dinner and other activities, his demeanor and attitude brightened considerably.

One place he really enjoyed going to was to the home of my mom's sister who lived close by. Aunt Eithel and dad often shared supper together. They both had lost someone they each loved, and they could reminisce about the good times, talk about their loss, and share the hope they had in Jesus.

• • • • •

When she gave out of her own need, the
chains of loneliness seemed lighter.

• • • • •

Kissing the chains of loneliness can be done in many ways. Doing things with family and friends is a great step. Another way to defeat the gnawing discouragement loneliness can foster is to find someone who needs to be encouraged—and then meet that need. We had a neighbor, Mary Williams, who did this wonderfully.

When we moved onto her street, Heidi and Nathan were very small. It wasn't long before she fell in love with our kids, and they fell in love with her. They would sometimes take her flowers...from her own garden! She didn't care too much for that gesture, but she never let the kids know it.

Mary was keen enough to see the look of desperation that came upon Steve and me sometimes as we dealt with the rigors of parenting youngsters. As a way of helping us out, she offered to sit with the children early in the morning so we could take walks together. She would read her paper and make sure they were safe, which gave us a much-needed hour to spend together. As a young married couple we were supremely grateful for her investment in our lives. She helped us, and in so doing she also helped herself. Mary's widowhood had became her opportunity to bless others. She discovered that when she gave out of her own need, the chains of loneliness seemed lighter and less restrictive.

Chained to "The Change"

"Menopause feels like a cage—a hot cage...no, a cold cage." I chuckled when I read this response to the question on personal chains. For many women, menopause is no laughing matter. Physical suffering doesn't always involve disease or injury. Sometimes the suffering is an unavoidable by-product of time. The natural process of aging brings suffering and dread. Experiencing the sudden ups and downs that come with menopause can be a big challenge. Though change is usually a formidable foe for all of us, if we want to live a peace-filled life we have to discover how to kiss even this chain.

Many books have been written on how to cope with the manifestations and limitations of menopause. I'll leave that kind of advice to the experts. However I want to encourage those of you who are going through this experience. You can face it with courage and live through it with wisdom.

As I approached this ominous time in my life, I said to Steve, "This is not your fault. You didn't cause this, and I will do my best to not blame you or punish you for something you can't fix." Then I made two requests. "First of all, don't ask any questions, and second, don't make any jokes about what you might be observing. I can joke, but you can't." He agreed, and he's been very good about it even though he struggles to understand it.

I recall one specific morning after a fitful, non-sleeping, sweaty night. I was sitting in front of the fireplace, rocking in a chair, and staring into the flames. Steve came into the room and saw me. In his sweet, kind voice he asked, "Whatcha thinkin' about?" I replied, "I think my thermostat is broken, and they are not making replacement parts for models my age." His first reaction was to look at the wall to see if the heating and cooling system unit in the house was malfunctioning. Then he suddenly stopped as he realized what I was talking about. He quietly whispered, "Oh." And that was the end of the conversation.

I've tried to not involve my family in my journey of "the change" because I don't want them to feel responsible for me and the chains menopause brings. My husband, my children, my friends, and my co-workers haven't done this to me. It's not their fault, and they can't do anything about the misery I'm experiencing. Furthermore, they don't deserve to be punished or to suffer for it. However, I do ask them to lend me their support by giving me their silence on the subject. I need them to give me some room and time to deal with the changes in my own private way. That's how I've chosen to kiss my chains.

Not everyone chooses to suffer in silence. Some women approach this time of change by wanting their families to be involved, supportive, and knowledgeable about how they feel, what they are thinking, and what they're experiencing. That's fine. Whatever works for you and your family is okay…as long as it's positive.

Unfortunately, I've also observed women who force their families to suffer with them. Every irritation is given a voice, every sleepless night is exposed, every sweaty episode is rehashed, and every ounce of weight gained is moaned over.

The people who love us are concerned and care about the trials and tribulations of menopause, but they are limited in what they can do about it. The bottom line is that we have to go through this time. Whether we make it a positive time or a negative time depends on whether we choose to kiss the chains or kick the chains. The choice is up to us.

Now, would someone please turn the heat down? No, wait…turn it up!

Chained to a Less-than-satisfying Marriage

"I'm in a marriage that looks nothing like what we had years ago." Unfortunately, this admission is repeated far too many times by far too many spouses. Steve and I have heard this statement made by close friends—but we were encouraged by it. Why? Because we believe that when a couple recognizes and confesses their feelings of being dissatisfied in their marriage, that confession can serve to strengthen their relationship.

How can this possibly be true? How will this help a couple recapture the love that may have been lost or the good feelings that are perhaps hidden behind the mountain of the cares of life? The answer is found in the insights contained in Jesus' words to the church in Ephesus, as recorded in the second chapter of Revelation. Jesus first commended the Ephesians for what they were doing right. He said:

> I know your deeds and your toil and perseverance, and that you cannot endure evil men, and you put to the test those who call themselves apostles, and they are not, and you found them to be false; and you have perseverance and have endured for my name's sake, and have not grown weary (verses 2-3).

Did you catch all that? Jesus affirmed what they were doing correctly:

- You work hard and never quit.
- You don't associate with bad people or do bad things.
- You keep a close watch on your religious beliefs and keep your doctrine sound.
- You never tire of following Me and upholding My teachings.

But doing the right things was not enough. Jesus points out the one thing that will cause negative judgment to come:

But I have this against you, that you have left your first love.
Remember therefore from where you have fallen, and repent and do the deeds you did at first; or else I am coming
to you, and will remove your lampstand out of its place—
unless you repent (verses 3-4).

What was the terrible wrong that had been done in the hearts of
the members of the church at Ephesus? Jesus was basically telling the
church they had walked away from the very essence of their relationship with God. To paraphrase what Jesus was saying to His bride (His
followers): "You have lost sight of what knowing each other is all about.
It's all about love. That's what is important to Me. Having a firm commitment, doing good deeds, avoiding bad people, maintaining sound
doctrine, all those things are fine—but that's not why I want you to be
my bride. What I want is your love."

To be restored and avoid that terrible judgment there were three
things the believers at Ephesus needed to do:

- *Remember* how much they loved Jesus in the beginning.
- *Repent* by acknowledging they were sorry for losing the in-
  timacy of the relationship they had once enjoyed with God.
- *Return* to the deeds and fervor they used to have.

How can we apply this to a marriage today that feels like a chain instead of a cherished union? First, we follow the guide given to us in Revelation 2:5: "Remember from where you have fallen." That means we are
to recall the feelings of joy and happiness we had when we first met and
rediscover the special companionship and intimacy with our spouses.

Steve and I enjoy reminiscing about our early days together. Re-
calling what generated the initial sparks of love that set our hearts
aflame for each other those many years ago refreshes our feelings for
each day. Sometimes we return to the settings where the "first love"
fires were lit. For example, when we eat at the old "meat and three"
where we spent many hours courting and dreaming about our future
together, the love fire is stoked. Simply sitting in that familiar booth

inspires us to recall those youthful, carefree days of companionship, love, and passion.

Another thing that can help us return to our first love is to display some of our wedding photos and keep our wedding album in a place that can be easily accessed. Some couples have put those nuptial pictures away, storing them in the attic, in the back of a closet, or in the bottom of a box. That's not where they belong. Those moments of commitment should be viewed often and lovingly.

Steve and I were a part of the 70s, the hippie generation. That meant we didn't value "posed" pictures, so we didn't have very many photographs taken at our wedding. Thankfully a dear friend insisted on taking some still photos so we have some snapshots of our special day. For our thirty-fifth anniversary I took the little snapshots of our wedding, along with the few we took on our honeymoon, to a local photo counter and had enlargements made. When I got home, I put together what I call our "poor man's wedding album." Once I got started putting the pictures together, I didn't want to stop! I ended up with a huge album that chronicled each year of our marriage. As Steve and I thumb through each picture, we talk about how we were feeling and what was going on at the time. This transports us back to those early feelings of love and passion.

But remembering is not enough. When we see how far we've fallen from the days of all-consuming love, the need to repent for allowing other things to replace what God has called holy is easier to recognize. Here are some good questions to ask:

- What has stolen our focus from one another?

- Are we so wrapped up in making a living that it's killing our time with each other?

- Are we giving the lion's share of our lives to our jobs, or careers, or something else?

- Is our energy supply always depleted because we're spending most of our efforts taking care of the kids, the house, the yard, and the hobbies we love so there isn't much left over for our mates?

- Are we offering our spouses something akin to a balloon with all the air let out?

Repentance is more than feeling sorry for missing the mark. It also requires—no, *demands!*—action. We need to turn away from the distractions and focus on our marriages again.

Once we have *remembered* and *repented,* the next step is to *redo* the things that sparked those early flames. This song lyric by Steve reflects what he heard a mother tell her son when asked for advice about his marriage that had lost the fire of first love.

Love Her Back Home

Mama, I'm calling you 'cause a woman knows what to do.
I'm alone in this big old house tonight.
Jenny says she don't care.
She's gone; she's out there somewhere.
What can I do to make it right?

And she said, "Get your keys, son. Get in that car.
Leave your pride behind and take a humble heart.
It doesn't matter if it takes all night long,
Find that woman. Son, find that woman,
And love her back home.

Take along those tender words,
the ones that she heard,
Back when she was all you dreamed about.
Take along that tender touch,
the one that means so much,
When a woman is dealing with the doubt.

And son, if you want her back,
I've told you everything you need.
'Cause it's what your father had with him,
when he looked all night for me.

Get your keys, son. Get in your car.
Leave your pride behind and take a humble heart.
It doesn't matter who's right or wrong.
Find that woman. Son, find that woman,
And love her back home.[2]

Steve's mother, Lillian, offers some profound wisdom when it comes to having a marriage that is honoring to Christ and satisfying to a husband and wife. Since she and P.J. have been married for more than 63 years, I perk up when she offers wisdom on keeping a marriage rock solid. Lillian says, "Born-again people get along." Isn't that simple? When we who call ourselves Christ-followers live according to God's Word and pursue the example of Jesus' servant heart, we will find ways to live together in harmony.

Are You Kissing or Kicking?

"How's life treating you?" is, to say the least, a loaded question for someone who might be feeling the cold, metallic chains of suffering. Their answer will often quickly reveal whether or not they are kissing or kicking the chains they are bound with. If you were asked that question, what would your answer be? Would someone hear you recounting in detail the woes of your life? If so, you are likely kicking the chains. And they will know it as well. However, if you have found the purpose in those chains, your answer will probably be filled with an infectious joy. According to Proverbs 17:22, "A joyful heart is good medicine, but a broken spirit dries up the bones."

If your emotional and spiritual bones are brittle, the people around you might also be inadvertently affected by any negativity you show or express.

I hope this brief look at a few of the chains that can bind us will help you look for the purpose in your chains and enable you to find hope and even joy in your trials. I pray that as a result of this chapter and book, you might need fewer antidepressants, anti-arthritis medicines, antacids, and pain-alleviating aids.

13

Choosing to Be Happy

Have you heard of the book *Everything I Ever Really Needed to Know I Learned in Kindergarten?* Well, I can go one better than that! One of the key lessons of life I learned from a *pre*-kindergartener.

One day my daughter, Heidi, and her little girl Lily came to my house for an overnight visit. Before we knew it, the day had ended and it was time for my sweet granddaughter, who was three years old at the time, to go to bed. As the bedtime ritual began, Heidi cheerfully informed Lily that she needed to brush her teeth. By Lily's reaction you would have thought her mother had just threatened to pull her teeth out instead of doing something that had been a part of their nighttime routine since her little pearlies popped through her gums. As evidenced by her reaction, my granddaughter is not one to do anything halfheartedly.

Lily began what would become a complete emotional and physical meltdown. The little darling began her tantrum by screaming at the top of her very young and very expansive lungs. She then kicked like a bucking bronco and clamped her mouth tighter than a hungry alligator with a mouth full of frogs. Although I was shocked and appalled by my sweet, can-do-no-wrong granddaughter's reaction, her mother was not surprised in the least. Evidently Heidi had witnessed this side of my little grand-blessing on more than one occasion. She was determined to not give in to Lily's youthful tirade. However, Lily had decided that this was her "Little Big Horn" of battles and she was not going down without a fight.

Although Heidi's reaction was totally different than the approach I would have taken, I decided I would be a good mother/grandmother and do the right thing. With the biblical imperative to not "spare the rod and spoil the child" wanting to fall from the tip of my tongue I stepped away from the situation and out of the room, although I stood where I could watch Heidi handle it.

• • • • • •

Even when things don't go the way I want
them to, I don't have to be held prisoner
to the downturn of emotions.

• • • • • •

In a calm, quiet voice I heard Heidi explain to Lily that her behavior was unacceptable. She made it clear what Lily was doing was wrong and then discussed the consequences of her actions.

"You have a choice. Choice number one is that you can obey me, brush your teeth, and be happy. Choice number two is that you can obey me, brush your teeth, get a spanking, and need a bucket." (When Lily gets upset she yells, "I need a bucket," as though she is threatening to throw up. Yes, she's my little drama queen.)

Heidi went on. "If you chose number two, you will be miserable and face the consequence of not enjoying your visit with DeDe and PaPa. But if you choose number one, you choose to obey what I've asked you to do, and you choose to be happy with your choice."

Right before my eyes I watched as a three-year-old did what I had never even considered an option. She calmed herself down, and after a few moments she looked up at her mother and held up one little finger. She had made the choice to not only brush her teeth, but to be happy about it! Though her eyes were still red and her face was still wet with the remnants of a well-fought battle, she managed to smile a little as she willingly brushed her tiny teeth. She'd decided to "kiss the chains" of parental authority.

Watching this tiny chain-kisser challenged me. I don't know if Lily was intrigued with the idea that we can make a choice and then be happy about it, but I certainly was. I'm not sure why it took me so long to figure out that not only can I choose to control my emotions, but I can also choose to be happy about it. What a revelation! That even when things don't go the way I want them to, I don't have to be held prisoner to the downturn of emotions that might follow. Nor do I have to let my emotions run their course so that the good feelings cycle back around, so to speak.

I immediately put this life-changing discovery to work. When I was mad at Steve, I always assumed I had no choice but to wait until my anger dissipated or was "out of my system" before I could feel right toward him again. I thought it was necessary to let a few hours pass—sometimes even a few days!—before I could forgive him or ask him to forgive me. From Lily I learned that I didn't have to be ruled by my emotions. Instead, I could be master over them. In essence, when it comes to choosing to embrace the chains of the unchangeable, I am better off acting more like a three-year-old! And this makes me smile as I remember that I am God's child, and He loves me enough to give me a choice of how to respond.

Turn 4

"Cleanse your hands."

14

Living in Freedom

*When you spread out your hands in prayer, I will
hide My eyes from you; yes, even though you multiply
prayers, I will not listen. Your hands are covered with
blood. Wash yourselves, make yourselves clean; remove
the evil of your deeds from My sight. Cease to do evil.*

Isaiah 1:15-16

Have you noticed how extremely important the nearness of God
and His life-changing presence are? Only He can help you deal
effectively with the many chains that bind you. Only He can reveal the
eternal purpose of those chains. With God as your strength, the next
turn toward wholeness and holiness awaits. You're ready to go from
"the chains to the stains."

Of all that can stain "the hands of the heart," there is one that can
lead to long-term effects if not corrected. And if it is corrected, it can
potentially release the majority of chain-bound people. What is this
tremendously powerful stain? Unforgiveness. Considering the sad condition people find themselves in as a result of withholding forgiveness,
I don't think we realize how polluted our hearts, minds, and hands get
or how much damage our bodies endure as a result of unforgiveness.

The Key to the Door

Jesus understood how important forgiveness is. When He was asked
by His disciples to teach them how to pray, of all the matters of life that

could have been addressed, forgiveness was among the few He mentioned. In Matthew 6:12 Jesus says to include this in your prayer: "And forgive us our debts." This is the door, so to speak, to enjoying God's divine favor. To open that door we need the key. Jesus included that too: "As we also have forgiven our debtors [those who have sinned against us]."

What does "forgive us our debts" refer to? Sin. The New Testament uses at least five different words to account for the variety of how we can fall or deliberately step into sin:

- *Hamartia.* This is an ancient archery term that carries the idea of "missing the mark." Sin causes our arrows of behavior to hit outside the target of God's bull's eye of righteousness.

- *Paraptoma.* This indicates slipping or falling. It refers to sin more from carelessness than from an intentional disobedience.

- *Parabasis.* This sin type is more conscious and intentional than "missing the mark" or "slipping or falling."

- *Anomia.* This means "lawlessness," and indicates an intentional or flagrant sin. It is direct and open rebellion against God and His ways.

- *Opheilema.* Most of the uses of this in verb form refer to moral or spiritual debts. Sin is a moral and spiritual debt to God that must be paid.[1]

To carefully emphasize His point, Jesus went on to say, "If you forgive others for their transgressions, your heavenly Father will also forgive you. But if you do not forgive others, then your Father will not forgive your transgressions" (Matthew 6:14-15). Looking at those five terms used in the original Greek of the New Testament, it's easy to see how we all fall short of God's ideal.

Why would Jesus ask us to forgive first, even before we are forgiven for a specific sin? Could it be that suffering through the gall of forgiving others for their sins against us is God's way of helping us better understand the anguish He endured on our behalf so we could obtain salvation and an intimate relationship with God? Although at first glance this comparison may seem trite or nonsensical, remember that sometimes forgiveness causes us to stretch beyond what we thought we could possibly experience or endure. Like you, I've experienced some harsh circumstances, and my thanks for Christ's sacrifice on the cross for the forgiveness of my sins runs deeper than it might have had I not tasted the sometimes bitter taste of struggling to forgive.

Though we can in no way comprehend the incredible suffering Christ went through to restore our relationship with God, we can and do get small tastes of His agony. My forgiveness journey began in earnest when I was only five years old.

In my book *Letting Go of Anger,* I candidly reveal that I was molested by a farmhand. As you would expect, this left a huge, open wound in my heart. Throughout my teen years and into college, I frankly deemed that despicable person's actions totally unforgivable.

The Physical Price of Unforgiveness

Unfortunately, unforgiveness eventually exacts a physical, emotional, and spiritual toll. My childhood was blotted with pain and misery of all kinds. From the age of five years old until my early twenties, I suffered excruciating, debilitating joint pain. I missed many of my elementary school days because I couldn't get dressed in the mornings. The joints in my shoulders would lock up, and I would writhe in agony. There were times when my body would become so swollen I ached. For example, the day I was measured for my high school class ring, my fingers were so enlarged that I ordered a size 10 ring. My normal finger size is 6.

When I was 12, Mother finally took me to the doctor to see if anything could be done about my condition. After a quick examination, the physician said that I had rheumatoid arthritis. He predicted I would most likely be in a wheelchair by the time I was 21. Although he offered medicine to dull the pain, you can imagine how devastating this diagnosis was to my family and me.

My body was crying out, "Something is terribly wrong! You have been hurt. You need to be healed." But no one was really listening, and no one understood so the torture continued. Psalm 6:2 says, "Be gracious to me, O LORD, for I am pining away; heal me, O LORD, for my bones are dismayed."

The Emotional Price of Unforgiveness

Along with the arthritis in my joints, the doctor recognized that I had some psychological issues that needed to be addressed. He suggested I be put on "nerve" medicine. (Back then, in the early 1960s, doctors didn't generally prescribe high-powered antidepressants or other pharmaceuticals to children, so this was a concession to the severity of my symptoms.) I was just a kid, yet somehow I knew that numbing the pain wasn't the answer to my problems. I'm not sure how I was aware of this, but I knew no pill could fix what was broken inside me. I refused to take the medicine, and I also refused to go back to that doctor. And my parents let it be my choice.

By the time I reached 16, I was in even worse shape. The physical pain was only matched by the emotional anguish I endured every day. I feared I was losing my mind. Looking back now, I know that God was holding me together. Colossians 1:17 says, "[Jesus] is before all things, and in Him all things hold together."

My emotions were on edge. The infected wound in my soul spread and seething rage filled my heart. At the least provocation I would inwardly and outwardly explode. I was exhausted and overwhelmed by the renegade emotions that dominated my life.

The Spiritual Price of Unforgiveness

Along with the physical and emotional pain, I also suffered spiritually. From my youngest years I had a true desire to know and love God. Although I had very little Bible knowledge and a limited understanding of God, I longed to be loved and accepted by Him. I also had a heightened awareness of my own sinfulness. Perhaps having been sinned against as a little girl, I understood the ugliness and destructive nature of sin. Also, I believe the physical and emotional suffering I went through gave me an extra measure of spiritual sensitivity. That acute awareness was especially revealed in my preteen years when I attended our little country church on a regular basis.

The pastor would preach his traditional Sunday morning sermon and end it with an appeal to those in the pews: "If anyone here has sinned this week, come forward and receive Christ and receive forgiveness for your sins." Now, you would think with such a broad, all-encompassing invitation, the altar would have been filled with people elbowing their way to the front of the line. Every week I thought, *If I sinned this week? Who hasn't? Of course I sinned.* But strangely enough, each time I heard the invitation, I was the only one who went to the altar to receive Christ and His forgiveness. And I did this every Sunday. Evidently the pastor was getting complaints from the church members. My going forward, praying, and crying every week was prolonging the church service. Consequently, there were disgruntled members of the congregation who didn't care for the way my responses to the altar calls were keeping them from getting home at the expected time. Perhaps their Sunday noon meal was being delayed or maybe the pot roast was getting a bit too dry. For whatever reason, I became the bane of their benediction schedule.

I learned later (through the gossip grapevine) that as a result of the grumbling, my Sunday school teacher was asked to take me aside and speak to me. In a back pew the next Sunday, she sat me down and said in a voice that was barely above a whisper, "When you go forward every week and cry and pray, people think you're doing," she paused and looked around to make sure no one was listening and then added the word bomb, "bad things."

Well, you didn't have to hit me over the head with a bat to get the idea through that "bad things" really meant "b-a-a-a-a-d things!" Suffice it to say, that was the last week I went forward.

Although I still carried the guilt-burden of being a dirty, rotten sinner, I did what the rest of the people in our congregation obviously did—ignored my pitiful spiritual state. While my heart became more hardened to sin, the physical and emotional damage was getting more difficult to control and live with. Though I kept trying, I found no relief. The rheumatism worsened, and my insides churned daily with bitterness. My nights were filled with unrest. I was tired of fighting the effects of pain and rage. But, praise the Lord, a true friend helped me face and fight my battle for freedom from the agony of the past. I did find release; however, it was the most difficult thing I've ever had to do.

Freedom!

When I was 21 and attending the Institute in Basic Youth Conflicts seminar conducted by Bill Gothard, I realized a life-altering truth: Much of my physical, emotional, and spiritual problems came back to the issue of unresolved woundedness and bitter unforgiveness. The reality that the things that happen to us in our past have a direct bearing on life in the present was a new revelation. When I faced that sad truth, my mind returned to the farm where I grew up. On the side of the hill above our house was a vivid picture of what my heart really looked like. It was a farm pond used mostly to water the cattle and occasionally to host a Sunday afternoon rock-skipping contest.

If you've ever been around a small body of water like our pond, you know that it can be quite deceiving. The water looked clear and clean on the surface. However, if we stepped into the water or took a long stick and stirred the bottom, it didn't take long to realize that it wasn't a healthy environment. Just a few feet below the surface of the water was muck and mire of all kinds. The stench of the stagnant, rotting materials on the floor was a disgusting indicator that there was not a sufficient and fresh source of water coming into the pond. At the bottom were decomposing debris, old tires, beer cans, junked car parts, and all manner of rubbish. The surface looked peaceful and calm, but underneath the real truth was told.

As I listened to the teachings offered by Bill Gothard, I knew my life resembled that farm pond. On the surface of my personality I might have seemed calm and tranquil. However, underneath the thin veneer were abscessed wounds made worse by years of unforgiveness and a bitter desire for revenge. I didn't want to be that way, but with no one to teach me how to change, I didn't know what to do. I didn't know why or how to forgive.

• • • • •

To know how to forgive opens the
door to discovering a life free from the
captivity of renegade emotions.

• • • • •

One day Aleta, my roommate in college, decided to do something for me that I was unwilling to do for myself. There was a very good reason for her loving action. She had a front-row seat to the wreck my life had become. Tired of hearing me hyperventilating and dry-heaving in the middle of the night, she made arrangements for me to see a counselor who worked at the Bill Gothard headquarters. The counseling center was located in a nearby suburb of Chicago where Aleta and I were attending school. She not only made the appointment with the counselor, but she also borrowed a car from a friend to take me there. When we arrived at the building she made me get out and walk into the office while she waited for me.

I will always be indebted to Aleta for being so proactive. She was like the friends of the paralytic who are mentioned in the second chapter of Mark. Unable to help himself, the paralyzed man was taken by his friends to Jesus. We read in the well-known account that being unable to get to Jesus because of the crowd, they removed the roof above Him; and when they had created an opening, they let down the pallet on which the paralytic was lying. And Jesus, *seeing their faith,* forgave and healed the man. It was as though Jesus recognized Aleta's faith just as he took note of the faith of the friends of the paralytic. And because of my friend's believing, the Healer turned His attention to my pathetic condition.

During what was supposed to be a 30-minute session (that turned into a much longer one), the counselor shared with me why and how to forgive. I don't remember the name of the man who helped me that day. I wish I could contact him and thank him for supplying the tools God used to tear down the stronghold of bitterness and unforgiveness and to help me build a life worth living. To know how to forgive opens the door to discovering a life free from the captivity of renegade emotions.

Granting Forgiveness

I never tire of sharing the life-changing information God used to set me free from the bondage of bitterness and the tyranny of unforgiveness. The four-step approach to forgiving the unforgivable that I was taught on that amazing day in the counselor's office may seem simple, but it is in no way easy. It's sort of like bench-pressing 200 pounds. Watching someone do it makes it look easy, but when you try it yourself, you suddenly understand the effort it takes.

It only took a few minutes for the counselor to share the concepts on how to forgive, and I felt some results rather quickly. However, achieving and maintaining forgiveness takes a lifetime. Why? I like the answer in the old saying I heard years ago: "The problem with a living sacrifice is it keeps crawling off the altar." The problem with forgiveness is found in the *inconsistency of the forgiver.*

I've used these same four steps to forgive the most egregious of wounds as well as the slightest of offenses. The authority of these steps comes because they are grounded in God's Word. If you follow these steps and don't allow yourself to become weary in well doing, you will discover freedom from the prison of unforgiveness and the chains of bitterness.

How to Forgive

1. *Stop pretending and start being honest.* When I first surrendered my heart to Jesus, I quickly believed that if I wanted to be accepted by other Christians I should start acting like one. That logic might sound like a pretty good idea, but it wasn't a viable plan at all. Truthfully, "acting like a Christian" destroyed any sense of honesty between me and the Lord. My feeble human attempts at making myself acceptable to Him lead to an insidious form of pride. And that pride created a hyper spiritual persona I tried very hard to keep up.

Maintaining the "good Christian girl" veneer meant acting religious and trying to be holy. It took me far too long to come to terms with the fact that God is not impressed with a pretense of piety. He loves His children enough to want them to be honest with Him. Nothing broken can be fixed unless the fracture is admitted and submitted to the heavenly Fixer. Pretending I was okay kept me from truly being okay for a long time.

When it came to my desperate need to find release, I needed to stop acting like I hadn't been offended. I had to recognize and voice my hurt and need for healing to God. I had to set aside my fear and shame of being judged by others and make myself vulnerable to the Great Physician. I had to give Him free access to the wounds festering in my heart and spirit. When I finally started being honest with God and admitted just how broken I was, He started the healing process and put me back together.

2. *Turn your thoughts into prayers.* Being honest with God is the first step toward healing. Venting old grievances and crying out to God from an honest heart is where we must *start*. However, if all we did was to be honest with God about our feelings, it would have about as much lasting effect as pounding our fist against a brick wall. It might make us feel better for the moment, but after a while we would be in worse shape than when we started.

The covering of denial and piety inhibits the healing process and provides the perfect breeding ground for infection. Turning our thoughts and feelings into prayers for help is like stripping off the old crusted dressing and cleaning the wound.

When we cry out to God for healing, our heavenly Father answers that prayer. Exodus 22:27 says, "When he cries out to Me, I will hear him, for I am gracious." We must give an honest accounting of how we feel about the offense and not worry about being nice. What exactly should we be praying for? A change of heart and a change of mind!

3. *Devour God's Word.* The Bible is not merely a coffee-table decoration. It is living, active, and sharper than a two-edged sword to

penetrate the heart and spirit and discern your thoughts. If you are not actively "eating" God's Word, you will never permanently achieve the change you so desperately need. Turning over a new leaf may be okay for some situations, but it isn't strong enough to handle something as difficult as forgiving a hurtful offense.

What does God's Word say about forgiving?

- "For if you forgive others for their transgressions, your heavenly Father will also forgive you. But if you do not forgive others, then your Father will not forgive your transgressions" (Matthew 6:14-15).

- "Why do you look at the speck that is in your brother's eye, but do not notice the log that is in your own eye? Or how can you say to your brother, 'Let me take the speck out of your eye,' and behold, the log is in your own eye? You hypocrite, first take the log out of your own eye, and then you will see clearly to take the speck out of your brother's eye" (7:3-5).

- "Then Peter came and said to Him, 'Lord, how often shall my brother sin against me and I forgive him? Up to seven times?' Jesus said to him, 'I do not say to you, up to seven times, but up to seventy times seven'" (18:21-22).

- "Whenever you stand praying, forgive, if you have anything against anyone, so that your Father who is in heaven will also forgive you your transgressions" (Mark 11:25).

- "Do not judge, and you will not be judged; and do not condemn, and you will not be condemned; pardon, and you will be pardoned. Give, and it will be given to you. They will pour into your lap a good measure—pressed down, shaken together, and running over. For by your standard of measure it will be measured to you in return" (Luke 6:37-38).

As I began to devour God's Word, He changed me from the inside out. Where hatred once flourished, love began to grow. Where anger robbed me of energy, peace found a resting place. I could feel myself changing as I became more and more knowledgeable about God's truths.

4. *Pray for your offender to come to a saving knowledge of Christ.* The fourth step would have been impossible had I not been diligent to do the first three. *Being honest with God* gave me the freedom to unburden my heart of the weight of the offense. *Turning my thoughts to prayer* gave me the strength to carry my burdens to the Lord and leave them there. *Filling my heart with God's Word* replaced the negative thought patterns that had dominated my thinking. Now I needed to take the final step in breaking the chain of unforgiveness. I had to decide if I would pray for my enemy. At this point I couldn't love him, but I did choose to pray for him. As I began to follow-through in obedience on this fourth step, I realized a truth that is absolute: *"I cannot consistently and earnestly pray for someone and maintain a hatred toward him or her."*

Praying for the man who nearly destroyed my life was extremely hard. I wanted my offender to pay—and pay big—for what he had done to me. Honestly, I wanted him to go to hell and burn forever. I thought, *If hell isn't for people like him, then what good is it?* However, as God's Word penetrated my heart and transformed my thinking, I began to see the man in a different light. God showed me that my offender wasn't the only one who warranted hell as his final resting place. I too deserved punishment. I hadn't committed the same sins as the man who violated me, but just like him, I was in need of forgiveness for things I had done…and things I had failed to do.

If I wanted God to have mercy on me and not give me what I deserved, then I needed to extend forgiveness to the people who wronged me. Basically, I had to come to the understanding that God would give my offender the same deal He was offering me. And I needed to draw on God's strength and love to extend mercy and grace to the rapist. Only when I recognized my own need for forgiveness and mercy was I able to contemplate…and eventually offer…that same grace to the person who violated me. The truth is that we both deserved judgment, but God, in His great love, chose to grant us mercy. I heard it put this way: "Grace is receiving what you *don't deserve*. Mercy is not receiving what you *do deserve*."

Innocent or Monster?

When I went in to see the counselor, we both sensed we had a limited time to talk so we were brutally honest. I told him how much I hated the person who had violated me, and I candidly shared how I longed for him to be eternally punished. And then I revealed my bottom-line perspective: "I was an innocent little child, and he was a horrible monster." Suddenly there it was, right there on the table of truthfulness for both of us to see. The ultimate unfairness of the offense.

The counselor, willing to go straight to the heart, said to me, "Who was the monster in your story? Was it the man who fed his sick lust by taking advantage of a little child or was the real monster the all-powerful, fully sovereign God who allowed such a horrible thing to happen to you?"

I was shocked at such a question. How could a man who claimed to be a Christian say such a thing? I reeled from the stunning blow that he thought I would accuse God of such complicity. But then I thought, *Could it be true? Could I really be angry at God? How could I be angry with God? I love Him.*

I had loved the Lord from the first time I heard that He loved me. God was the One I tried to please. The One I was supposed to serve. Was my real grievance with the Lord, whom I professed to love, rather than the instrument of evil who perpetrated the actual offense? Suddenly the question was too obvious to ignore. How did an all-knowing, all-powerful, all-loving, just God let something so hideous happen to an innocent child?

After we talked a bit more, the counselor pointed out that God could have stopped what happened, but He didn't. Then he asked, "What are you going to do with this knowledge?"

I left the counseling session that day with that specific question unanswered. But thankfully, after much soul searching, I finally came to terms with my anger situation. I realized the challenging fact that as long as I looked at life from an innocent/monster point of view, I would never forgive. And if I didn't forgive, I would continue to be held captive by the brutal taskmaster of bitterness.

To correct the error of the innocent/monster mindset I'd been holding on to with a tight fist, the Holy Spirit opened my eyes to an important truth: As long as I saw myself as the innocent and my offender as the monster, I would never be able to forgive the man for his sin against me. Why? Because the chasm between an innocent and a monster is a gap too wide to span with the bridge of forgiveness. Even the secular world of counseling recognizes this "gap truth." They know that the wide divide between the perpetrator and the victim must be closed. In order to do so, the secular view raises the perpetrator to make him or her closer to an innocent. They offer excuses and "reasons":

- He was under the influence of alcohol and drugs.
- He never had a daddy in the home.
- He came from an impoverished situation.
- He was abused as a child.
- He's not responsible for what he did.
- It's not his fault. He was genetically predisposed to violence.

While this seeks to make the monster an innocent victim so the gap is narrowed, look at how God's Word closes the gap for forgiveness to take place. With each of the following realities, the gap is closed as we realize we all have sinned:

- "In sin my mother conceived me" (Psalm 51:5).
- "Our righteous deeds are like a filthy garment" (Isaiah 64:6).
- "From within, out of the heart of men, proceed the evil thoughts, fornications, thefts, murders, adulteries, deeds of coveting and wickedness, as well as deceit, sensuality, envy, slander, pride and foolishness. All these evil things proceed from within and defile the man" (Mark 7:21-23).
- "There is none righteous, not even one" (Romans 3:10).
- "All have sinned and fall short of the glory of God" (Romans 3:23).

The resulting picture, from God's point of view, is that there are no monsters and no innocents in my story. Instead, there are two pitiful, helpless, desperate, sin-sick souls in need of redemption through Jesus Christ. Only when I saw myself as one who was also guilty before God could I forgive the one who had perpetrated evil against me.

And what a change has been wrought in my life since that time. Now, because the forgiveness of my offender has been worked out in my heart, instead of having a life that is reminiscent of a putrid farm pond, I enjoy the by-products of asking and allowing God to help me forgive. Because of Christ there is fresh water flowing daily into my "pond" that brings life. Jesus said, "If anyone is thirsty, let him come to Me and drink. He who believes in Me, as the Scripture said, 'From his innermost being will flow rivers of living water'" (John 7:37-38). This flow is the reward of choosing to forgive!

Forgiveness Means Freedom

I don't know what you've had to endure during your lifetime. You may never have had anything really terrible happen to you. If that is the case, I am very happy for you. However, I'm sure you've been wronged in some way.

When mankind made the choice to live independently of God's perfect plan, everything changed. Now we live in a damaged world filled with wounded people who have a propensity to inflict wounds on everyone around them. Having lived many years with the venom of unforgiveness poisoning my life, keeping my hands stained with bitterness, and knowing the deadness it brings, I strongly urge you to turn your back on bitterness and fully embrace the grace of God. He will help you walk through the hurt and harm that has been done to you. He will help you find your way to forgive those who have injured you.

You Were Called to Freedom

I once heard it said that the good news of the gospel is simply one beggar telling another beggar where to find bread. I love that! None of us has everything about life figured out. Not one of us is perfect or without fault. It must break God's heart to see His people—His creations—living wounded and hurting when He is right here wanting to fix what is broken. Listen to what Jesus came to do for us:

> The Spirit of the Lord GOD is upon me, because the LORD
> has anointed me to bring good news to the afflicted; He
> has sent me to bind up the brokenhearted, to proclaim liberty to captives and freedom to prisoners; to proclaim the
> favorable year of the LORD and the day of vengeance of our
> God; to comfort all who mourn, to grant those who mourn
> in Zion, giving them a garland instead of ashes, the oil of
> gladness instead of mourning, the mantle of praise instead
> of a spirit of fainting. So they will be called oaks of righteousness, the planting of the LORD, that He may be glorified. Then they will rebuild the ancient ruins, they will raise
> up the former devastations; and they will repair the ruined
> cities, the desolation of many generations (Isaiah 61:1-4).

We long for peace and freedom. Yet because we continue to try to find it on our own and go through life alone, we keep coming up short. By the grace of God, Jesus came to bring good news to us all! His willingness to forgive us is the best of all news. And our willingness to forgive others as we have been forgiven is part of the divine duet we are privileged to participate in.

More Good News

Here is more good news for wounded travelers. As a result of the finished work of Christ and His redemptive power in our lives...

- we are more than what we have done.
- we are more than what has been done to us.

We are called to be free in Christ. That, my friend, is wonderful news! Are you free from the bondage of the past? If you aren't, there is hope in Christ! I can testify joyfully that you can be like I am even though you and I are far from perfect on our own. I'm thankful that...

- I am free from the bitterness that once dominated every area of my life.

- I am free to accept and offer forgiveness to those around me.

- I am free from the exhausting job of judging and condemning others.

- Being forgiven and forgiving others has helped free me from the crippling unrest and painful disease that once racked my body.

- I am free from the damage that once defined my existence.

- I am free of anger and the woundedness that tainted my soul.

- I am free to understand and accept the amazing mercy and grace from my loving God who offered forgiveness through Jesus Christ.

15

Setting Healthy Boundaries

There's hardly an act of obedience to God's Word more challenging yet more rewarding than offering forgiveness. Though this is true, forgiving is probably one of the most misunderstood choices a person can make. For that reason, let's take a closer look at forgiveness to see what it is and, just as important, what it is not. Webster's dictionary states that "to forgive" is to forget, excuse, pardon, let off (as in a criminal being released), to absolve, to exonerate. With these actions being the root meaning of being a forgiver, is it any wonder that offended victims find it so difficult, and in some cases nearly impossible, to forgive?

Some people say that unless the offender explicitly asks to be forgiven, people are under no obligation to forgive. But the Bible says just the opposite. Jesus forgave each of us long, long ago before we even knew to ask Him for forgiveness. In turn, even if an offender never asks us to forgive him or her, we need to follow God's example and extend forgiveness. Why should we follow His lead? For our spiritual and emotional freedom, for our peace of mind, and, for many of us, for the healing of our bodies.

To withhold forgiveness can have deadly consequences, an outcome that is well illustrated in an ancient tribal punishment for the crime of murder. It is said that centuries ago, when a person was convicted and sentenced for murder, the decaying body of the slain individual was chained to the back of the murderer. In a few days, which doubtless seemed an eternity to the convicted man, the rotting corpse he had slain would infect him and eventually kill him.[1]

When we refuse to forgive, we basically choose to carry around the rotting corpse of the offense everywhere we go. Eventually that unforgiveness will make us diseased and infected with bitterness and anger. Unforgiveness produces a broken spirit that becomes unable to receive or give grace. Unforgiveness also festers, infecting our physical bodies, resulting in crippling effects of stress and anxiety. We were never designed to carry such emotional and spiritual loads. Because of this, forgiving is actually the kindest thing we can do for ourselves and for those around us. Consider, for example, how forgiveness can benefit these offended ones:

- For incest victims, forgiving the perpetrators will liberate them from the prisons of shame and secrecy.

- For the victims of marital betrayals through the sin of adultery, forgiving their spouses gains release from an unholy alliance to bitterness and revenge.

- For physically, emotionally, and mentally abused people, forgiving their abusers/bullies breaks the chains of control and manipulation the perpetrators try to exert over their victims.

- For the people who have been unfairly slandered and maligned, forgiving the malicious gossipers silences the voices of the liars and restores peace.

If you can relate to one or more of these scenarios, or if there are any other situations that have left you offended, I pray you'll find the courage to forgive so you can experience the joy and healing that comes when the dead corpse of offense is lifted off your back. When you do, your life will drastically change for the better.

What Forgiveness Isn't

You know what forgiveness is and what benefits can be gleaned from it. But there are a few important principles about what forgiveness *is not*. You'll want to know these so you can avoid the traps the enemy of your soul will set for you during your life journey. We'll look at three of the critical things forgiveness is not.

Forgiveness **Is Not** *Forgetting*

How many times have we heard the cliché "You have to forgive and forget"? Some people believe these two are naturally linked together. Wouldn't that be terrific if it were true? Just think of what a relief it would be if we could choose to forgive and automatically the offense would be eliminated from our memories. Life would be so much more enjoyable if we could overlook every negative name we've been called, disregard every hurtful experience, and put out of mind any life-altering traumas that have taken place. Sadly though, life doesn't work that way—and neither do we. We don't possess a delete button on our hard drives.

Forgetting is a nice notion, but is that really what we want? When we expect people to forget something that took place we are, in essence, requiring them to choose amnesia, a serious medical condition. To forget a painful incident or situation that had a profound impact on our lives is not only impossible, it's not healthy. If we forget that something negative has happened, we won't guard against it in the future or take steps to decrease the effects. Total forgiveness does not involve forgetting what happened, but rather, to remember what happened without the debilitating pain. Not only does forgiveness allow us to recall the incident without the hurt that was once attached to it, but forgiving gives us the freedom to search for the good that God can bring out of the pain.

Example Is the Best Teacher

A good example of one who was able to forgive a series of horrible offenses and yet fully see the greater picture was the remarkable Jewish patriarch, Joseph. Most of us have heard the account of his life and all that he suffered. His life seldom fails to inspire those who have experienced mistreatment at the hands of others. Look at a few of the things that we know Joseph endured in the first four decades of his life:

- suffered the death of his beloved mother
- betrayed by his brothers as they plotted his murder
- sold into slavery by his brothers and subjected to forced labor in a foreign region
- deprived of the love of his father
- robbed of his Jewish heritage
- denied the use of his language
- stripped of the exercise of his religion
- fleeced out of his inheritance
- imprisoned unjustly
- abandoned by those he'd helped while in prison

Who wouldn't have been bitter after all Joseph had experienced? From the age of 17 until he was nearly 40, his life was marred by people who abused, maligned, slandered, imprisoned, and abandoned him. Yet as we read the account of his life, we find no hint of anger, self-pity, or unforgiveness. In fact, when he came into a position of power and could easily have indulged himself in retribution against his Egyptian owner Potiphar and his lying wife, there is no indication that he did. He could have exacted a pound of flesh from the ingrate cupbearer who forgot him in prison, but he did not. When he was finally reunited with his brothers who had sold him into slavery and stolen his life from him, he did not repay them in kind. In fact, everything about his life showed the opposite of an angry, vengeful person.

As a testimony to his outlook, consider the names Joseph gave to his sons. Manasseh: "For…God has made me forget all my trouble and all my father's household," and Ephraim: "God has made me fruitful in the land of my affliction" (Genesis 41:51-52).

As far as we can surmise from the biblical account, Joseph did not harbor unforgiveness and bitterness toward those who had hurt him. He had a clear conscience. The same can't be said for his sneaky brothers. They felt ashamed for what they'd done and feared he would punish them. Their guilt was quite evident when they recognized their brother and realized he was a man with great power and authority. They judged Joseph according to their own misguided inclinations. They said, "What if Joseph bears a grudge against us and pays us back in full for all the wrong which we did to him!" (Genesis 50:15). Fearing a payback that would trump their evil deeds, his brothers came and fell down before him, humbly saying, "Behold, we are your servants" (verse 18).

Joseph's response tells us volumes about who he was and how he regarded His God. "'Do not be afraid, for am I in God's place? As for you, you meant evil against me, but God meant it for good in order to bring about this present result, to preserve many people alive. So therefore, do not be afraid; I will provide for you and your little ones.' So he comforted them and spoke kindly to them."

Joseph was aware of what he'd lost by the sinful deeds of his brothers, but he made a deliberate choice to forgive. He was able to see that his brothers were not the ones who decided the path his life would take. Joseph fully trusted in a sovereign, all-powerful, loving God who would ultimately work everything together for good.

You may be thinking, *Well, Joseph is mentioned in the Bible as an example to us, so of course he responded correctly. I'm not a saint. There is no way that I can be expected to offer kindness and forgiveness to someone who severely does me wrong.* God's grace is not limited to those we know through the pages of the Bible. He is no respecter of persons. *His grace is sufficient for any who call on His name.*

A Modern-day Joseph

I can't imagine a more difficult thing to forgive than when someone injures a family member. In the book *A Grace Disguised,* Jerry Sittser shares his journey through the devastating loss of his wife, his mother, and his precious four-year-old daughter due to a tragedy involving a drunk driver. Jerry and his family were returning to their residence from a homeschool field trip they had taken to an Indian Reservation in Idaho. Their minivan was hit head-on by a heavily intoxicated driver, who was later acquitted of any legal responsibility on a technicality. The driver was going well over the speed limit when he crashed into Jerry's vehicle. The violent collision killed five people, three of them Jerry's family members. It threw Jerry's world into a tailspin that seemed like it would never stop turning. Remarkably, he and three of his children survived the crash, but they didn't walk away uninjured.

Jerry can't forget the tragedy that took the lives of his loved ones, and no one in their right mind expected him to. However, throughout his book the message of forgiveness is on each page. I was particularly moved by a dream Jerry wrote about in the midst of his unbelievable pain and loss.

> I dreamed of a setting sun. I was frantically running west, trying desperately to catch it and remain in its warmth and light. But I was losing the race. The sun was beating me to the horizon and was soon gone. I suddenly found myself in the twilight. Exhausted, I stopped running and glanced with foreboding over my shoulder to the east. I saw a vast darkness closing in on me. I was terrified by that darkness. I wanted to keep running after the sun, though I knew that it was futile, for it had already proven itself faster than I was. So I lost all hope, collapsed to the ground and fell into despair. I thought at that moment that I would live in darkness forever. I felt absolute terror in my soul.

After sharing this dream with his sister, she said,

> The quickest way for anyone to reach the sun and the light of day is not to run west, chasing after the setting sun, but to head east, plunging into the darkness until one comes to the sunrise.

Jerry then writes,

> I discovered in that moment that I had the power to choose the direction my life would head, even if the only choice open to me, at least initially, was either to run from the loss or to face it as best I could.[2]

Can you imagine the cruelty and the idiocy of saying to Jerry that in order for him to forgive the man who killed his family that he would have to forget the incident and the impact it had on him and the rest of his family? Of course not! Remembering something that happened is essential to forgiving what happened.

Forgiveness Is Not *Excusing*

One day after I finished speaking at a women's conference, a mother and her teenage daughter were waiting to talk to me. They shared that the young girl had been sexually abused by her father. The man was serving many years in prison for his crime against her. The mother was very upset that the girl was so damaged by what had happened to her. She wanted her daughter to be free, and she knew the only way for her to turn the tragedy into triumph was for her to forgive her father. However, after a brief conversation with them I discovered that the mother had fallen prey to an erroneous definition of forgiveness. She had confused forgiveness with "pardoning" or "exonerating" the perpetrator. The daughter revealed her misguided understanding of forgiveness when she confided, "If I forgive my dad, then it means what he did to me was all right."

Forgiving is not offering a pardon for wrongs that have been done. In fact, you can fully forgive and still want the person prosecuted for the offense. You can forgive and still testify against someone. Forgiving a person and recognizing the wrong or the illegality of what he or she has done are two separate issues. In fact, a victim can participate in the prosecution of an offender and still carry a heart of forgiveness into the courtroom.

One thing I've learned from television court shows is the limitations that victims have when it comes to righting the wrong done to them in a court of law. When a defendant is being tried for a crime, it is not the victim who brings the complaint to the court. The state is the prosecutor. Only "the state" has the power to try, convict, sentence, and punish an individual for a transgression of the law. Likewise, only the state can declare an individual not guilty of the crime. (The only recourse citizens have to remedy crimes committed against them is to sue in a civil court. The victim can seek to make the offender compensate him or her financially, but only the state can punish by taking away a person's freedom or life.)

We can personally extend forgiveness to people, forgiving them from our hearts, and they still will be held sin-guilty before God. Just as the state is the only one responsible to carry out justice in the legal system, so God is the only judge who can forgive and pardon sin. Our heavenly Father has been very kind to us taking on the heavy responsibility of dealing with sin and punishment. As fallen human beings, we are not qualified to pass judgment on one another. We need to be very careful when we demand justice instead of mercy. More than likely, although perhaps not in such harsh circumstances, there will come a time when we all have need of mercy. James 2:12-13 says, "So speak and so act as those who are to be judged by the law of liberty. For judgment will be merciless to one who has shown no mercy; mercy triumphs over judgment."

Forgiving Is Not *Necessarily Reconciling*

Forgiving someone does not mean you have to reconcile with them. If you forgive someone an offense, that doesn't mean you are required to allow that person back into your life or grant him or her access to your heart and mind. Of the three things that forgiveness is not, this is the most important. Great harm can result by believing that an offender should be welcomed back into someone's life. A good case in point is one story where a stepfather molested his stepdaughter.

• • • • •

Forgiveness is a command from
God; reconciliation is earned.

• • • • •

In an attempt to skirt the public embarrassment of such a heinous scandal, the family decided to "forgive" the stepdad. The assault became a family secret. They decided not to prosecute. Evidently they believed that the humiliation of being discovered and the contriteness of the man would be punishment enough and the man would stop the behavior. Did letting the stepfather off the hook for his criminal, immoral, and unthinkable behavior stop him from further offenses? Tragically, no. In fact, the stepfather kept molesting the stepdaughter and soon molested a granddaughter. Years passed and the family never put a stop to the betrayal…or stepped outside the family circle for help. When a great-granddaughter became addicted to drugs and was suicidal, it was learned that she too had been preyed on by that man. What finally put a stop to the molestation of the generations of women in that family? The offender died.

Forgiving doesn't mean we allow toxic, dangerous people to have access to us or our families. We must listen to the voice in our hearts (the Holy Spirit talking to us!), biblical principles, and our laws that require us to protect ourselves, protect those we love, and prevent such dangerous behavior from continuing.

Is reconciliation ever appropriate? Yes, but not without a lot of work, counseling, restoration of earned trust, and the implementation of safeguards. People make choices, and choices have consequences. Some decisions people make can result in that person not being allowed to be part of our lives. When people have shown they are untrustworthy, we need to keep them at a distance for our safety. When people have broken or shattered our trust, it is up to them to make the changes needed and then prove to us that they are trustworthy. Forgiveness is a command from God; reconciliation is earned.

When reconciling comes up, we need to look at the severity of the offense and what the possible repercussions are. Making the decision to reconcile with someone who has assaulted you takes a lot more thought, prayer, consultation, and counseling than when dealing with someone who has slighted you in some way, such as not saying hello or forgetting to return a phone call. Please be careful.

You don't want to allow a hurt that was the result of something inadvertent or nonlife-threatening to became so powerful that you choose to cut someone out of your life. Remember what Jesus said about offenses:

Why do you look at the speck of sawdust in your brother's eye [his or her petty offense against you] and pay no attention to the plank in your own eye [your unwillingness to recognize their offense as small and your own culpability to similar issues]? How can you say to your brother, "Brother, let me take the speck out of your eye," when you yourself fail to see the plank in your own eye? You hypocrite, first take the plank out of your eye and then you will see clearly to remove the speck from your brother's eye (Luke 6:41-42 NIV).

16

Seeking Forgiveness

If you have wronged someone, it is your responsibility to do whatever it takes to bridge the gap created by your actions or inactions. Let's look at the five steps to take for asking for forgiveness and the biblical reasoning behind them.

1. *Admit what you did was wrong.* Admitting and agreeing with God about our guilt is the first step necessary to knowing the peace that comes with receiving His forgiveness. First John 1:9-10 says, "If we confess our sins, He is faithful and righteous to forgive us our sins and to cleanse us from all unrighteousness. If we say that we have not sinned, we make Him a liar and His word is not in us." In the same way, to be reconciled to a person we have sinned against, we have to admit to them what we did was wrong.

Matthew 5:23-24 says: "If you are presenting your offering at the altar, and there remember that your brother has something against you, leave your offering there before the altar and go; first be reconciled to your brother, and then come and present your offering." These two verses make it very clear that we can go no further in achieving reconciliation with the person we have offended until we are willing to admit what we did was wrong.

2. *Apologize.* We should express remorse for what we have done. Nearly every day it seems like we hear a public apology from someone

in a prominent position who has fallen into sin's trap. Sometimes we hear an appeal for forgiveness from an athlete who has cheated his or her way to the victory podium. Sometimes politicians betray the trust of the public through moral failure. And we have witnessed the tearful, chin-quivering admissions from prominent Christian leaders who have espoused one standard of living for their congregation while living a secret life outside the biblical mandates.

None of us is perfect; we all fall short of the standards we set for ourselves and for others. That said, not all apologies, or confessions, or repentances are true and come from the heart. We need to learn the real meaning of repentance and make our honest confessions before God. One man who understood the depths of sin *and* the deliverance of repentance was King David. He was a man who knew how to apologize. Although this mighty man was referred to as the "apple of God's eye," he, like the rest of us, had to deal with his sinful failings and answer to the Lord for the consequences of his actions (2 Samuel 11).

While some of the public apologies we have witnessed are a mixture of making excuses and blaming others, King David gives an example of what a true apology should look like. To help you hear this message from in Psalm 51:1-17 with "fresh" ears, I'm going to quote from the New Living Translation. These steps of repentance before God are the same ones that need to accompany our apologies to the people we have sinned against.

A cry for forgiveness: "Have mercy on me, O God, because of your unfailing love. Because of your great compassion, blot out the stains of my sins. Wash me clean from my guilt. Purify me from sin" (Psalm 51:1-2 NLT).

A confession of sin: "For I recognize my rebellion; it haunts me day and night. Against you, and you alone, have I sinned; I have done what is evil in your sight. You will be proved right in what you say, and your judgment against me is just. For I was born a sinner—yes, from the moment my mother conceived me. But you desire honesty from the womb, teaching me wisdom even there" (verses 3-6).

An appeal for cleansing: "Purify me from my sins, and I will be clean; wash me, and I will be whiter than snow. Oh, give me back my joy again; you have broken me—now let me rejoice. Don't keep looking at my sins. Remove the stain of my guilt" (verses 7-9).

A plea for a second chance: "Create in me a clean heart, O God. Renew a loyal spirit within me. Do not banish me from your presence, and don't take your Holy Spirit from me. Restore to me the joy of your salvation, and make me willing to obey you" (verses 10-12).

A promise to help others: "Then I will teach your ways to rebels, and they will return to you. Forgive me for shedding blood, O God who saves; then I will joyfully sing of your forgiveness. Unseal my lips, O Lord, that my mouth may praise You. You do not desire a sacrifice, or I would offer one. You do not want a burnt offering. The sacrifice you desire is a broken spirit. You will not reject a broken and repentant heart, O God" (verses 13-17).

To recap, these are the steps to biblical repentance:

- a cry for forgiveness
- a confession of sin
- an appeal for cleansing
- a plea for a second chance
- a promise to help others

3. *Amend the situation.* Taking the third step of making restitution where possible is essential if we are going to ask for and be forgiven—and even possibly be reconciled to the person we have sinned against. Keep in mind that words are cheap, but actions show whether we really mean what we say and do.

A Tragic Reality

Some actions cannot be amended. There's a lot of truth in the adage, "You can't unring a bell." There are times when our only choice is to learn to live with what we've done and the consequences. There is no way, for instance, that a drunk driver who drives head-on into a school bus filled with laughing children, killing dozens of them, can make things right. Hopefully the state will do its job and the irresponsible driver will be punished, but nothing the driver can say or do will make up for the tragedy of loss the families and community will suffer. Thankfully, however, there are many offenses that can be amended. When making things right for the person you've wronged, there are a couple of guidelines to keep in mind.

It's Not Just About You

I recall one night when Steve and I were fast asleep. The phone rang, and with muddled mind and sleepy eyes, Steve struggled to find the phone. On the other end of the line was a familiar voice but it wasn't someone we talked to on a daily basis.

Gradually Steve realized what the caller was saying. He'd awakened us in the middle of the night to confess that he'd cheated us out of some money on a business transaction. He explained the circumstance, the amount he'd stolen, and how he was feeling terribly guilty over this sin.

After hearing him out, Steve responded that he understood and forgave him for the theft. Steve ended the call and hung up. He turned to me and explained the gist of the conversation.

I was irritated, but it had nothing to do with being robbed; it had everything to do with the guy's bad timing. "Why couldn't he have waited until morning?" I groused. There's no doubt *he* must have felt better after having confessed his sin, but we were left to deal with the adrenaline rush of confusion, dismay, aggravation, and possible repercussions. Getting back to sleep was extremely difficult!

Follow Through

After the midnight confession, we expected the money that had been stolen would be returned. However, we never heard another peep about the matter. Evidently paying back the money was not part the thief's making-amends process. So the caller's late-night call only accomplished one positive thing—relief for his guilt feelings. The confession seemed to be just as selfish as the thievery!

When people say, "I take full responsibility for what I have done" and then refuse to follow up their contriteness with a change of attitude or behavior as well as restitution, they aren't truly making amends. Words need to be followed with action:

- Have you stolen money? Make arrangements to repay it. No matter how long it takes, pay back every cent.

- Have you fathered or mothered a child you don't live with? Financially provide for the child. Child support is more than just a legal mandate. Go beyond what is legally required and give out of love—if not love for the child then love for God. You have a parental responsibility for the welfare of the child. And that includes being emotionally supportive too. Do you live far away from him or her? If possible, move closer so you can put feet and hands to your words and be actively involved in your offspring's life. Sending a check is not enough. You participated in the conception; you need to participate in the emotional development of the child. Spiritually, you also have a responsibility to teach your child about spirituality and share Jesus Christ. And if he or she becomes a believer, you have the responsibility to help him or her mature in God. If you don't have access to your child, you can at the minimum pray and fast on his or her behalf. Speak the words of God into your child's life. These steps are part of your making amends process.

• • • • •

Words do not make everything right. They
need to be followed with action.

• • • • •

- Have you gossiped about someone? Go to the person to whom you gossiped with and confess your sin. Tell him or her gossip is wrong and you're sorry you participated in it. Then go to the person you gossiped about and confess. Tell him or her that you sinned and admit that what you said was unkind (and unsubstantiated if that's the case). Contrary to what many people believe, gossip is not a victimless sin.

When people spread gossip, they are also maligning some-one's reputation or actions. We can never take back the sting of our inappropriate words, but we can own up to them and fix what we can.

4. *Aim to change your ways.* Commit to learning *why* you did what you have done. Also, determine what you need to do to change your behavior. The nature of the offense will determine what you need to do to fix it.

- Put yourself under the accountability of another person.
- Start going to church and submit to spiritual training.
- Go to a marriage counselor and find ways to fix what you've broken.
- Commit to changing what you say and how you say it to those around you.

5. *Ask for forgiveness.* The end result of admitting, apologizing, making amends, and changing behavior enables you to reasonably ask for forgiveness. You can't make someone forgive you, but you can do your part. God offers unconditional, perfect forgiveness; but humans aren't always quick to see and accept the good and the contrition in us. And they aren't always willing to extend a pardoning hand. And that's okay…and that's not your problem. The ultimate act of the other person granting you forgiveness is between him or her and God. Your part is to make it as easy as possible for the one whom you've offended to find it in his or her heart to want to forgive.

The peace of mind that comes to us through asking for forgiveness and being forgiven on a human level leads to the even greater joy of realizing anew the great act God has done to allow us to be forgiven for our sins and cleansed through the blood of His Son, Jesus Christ. Another adage I appreciate comes to play here: "There is no softer pillow than a conscience that is clear."

Turn 5

"Purify your heart."

17

Leaning on God's Grace

During the course of this book you've been introduced to four course corrections noted in James 4:7-8:

- Submit therefore to God.
- Resist the devil and he will flee from you.
- Draw near to God and He will draw near to you.
- Cleanse your hands, you sinners.

Be of good cheer, you have now reached the fifth turn this passage gives:

"And purify your hearts, you double-minded."

As mentioned early on, it is essential to understand that each turn or action be made in order. *Submitting our lives to God* and learning to participate with Him in the "divine duet" leads to the strength needed to *resist the destructive voices of the enemy.* Then, when God's voice is allowed to be the only sound we long to hear, *drawing near to Him* results in Him drawing near to us and helps us more clearly see His purpose for our lives, even if it sometimes involves chains. The growing relationship then gives us the assurance of knowing that He has not only forgiven us but will help us *cleanse our hands* by forgiving others. And then, on the basis of that confidence, we take the next turn of *purifying our hearts* so that we are never again unsure (double-minded), about the fact that we belong to God.

The word "purify" in the James 4 passage means to consecrate or set apart for God's use. The result of submitting, resisting, drawing near, and cleansing our hands is, in essence, complete surrender to God (consecration). Now it's time to talk to God about everything you've done through this process.

A Special Time with God

As a tangible way of saying to God that your heart is completely His, I suggest doing this simple exercise. You'll need these basic tools:

- a private, quiet place to talk to the Lord
- at least an hour of uninterrupted time
- a pen or pencil
- paper (3 to 5 sheets)
- a portable paper shredder

To get the most out of this process, determine ahead of time that you'll be completely honest with yourself and with God. Also bear in mind that no one will see what you write unless you decide to share.

Dealing with Guilt

Are you ready to begin? First, write your name and the date at the top of one of the sheets of paper. Now ask the Lord to bring to your remembrance any sin or sins that have weighed you down and that you feel guilty about. If you've confessed these transgressions previously yet they bother you, still write them down. Be sure to include the items that sometimes come to mind in the middle of the night when you wake up feeling nagging regret or gnawing dread.

Read this list out loud, letting God know that you realize these things have offended Him as well as hurt you and others. Thank Him for His mercy and His infinite forgiveness. Commit to your part in the divine duet by asking Him to show you how to replace these destructive thoughts and deeds with obedience.

Read the following verses and take a few moments to meditate on them:

> Do not let sin control the way you live; do not give in to sinful desires. Do not let any part of your body become an instrument of evil to serve sin. Instead, give yourselves completely to God, for you were dead, but now have new life. So use your whole body as an instrument to do what is right for the glory of God. Sin is no longer your master, for you no longer live under the requirements of the law. Instead, you live under the freedom of God's grace (Romans 6:12-14 NLT).

Dealing with Shame

Next write down everything that causes feelings of shame to rise up within you. Include the names you have called yourself or the labels others have used to hurt and define you. List everything you can think of regarding you and shame.

Now, going through your list, for each one consciously reject it as a lie. Tell God you're sorry for doubting His love and mercy toward you in this area (repenting). By faith, choose to *replace* the lies with the truths found in God's Word—that you are a beloved daughter of the King of kings. Praise His name for all He's done for you!

Dealing with Fear

Write down your greatest fears. What are the worries in your life that have become bigger than God? Confess them as sin and commit to putting your trust in God. By faith, you are "destroying speculations and every lofty thing raised up against the knowledge of God, and [you] are taking every thought captive to the obedience of Christ" (2 Corinthians 10:5-6). Where fear used to take up room in your mind, fill that place with God's truths, including these two passages:

> Do not let your heart be troubled; believe in God, believe also in Me. In My Father's house are many dwelling places;

if it were not so, I would have told you; for I go to prepare a place for you. I will come again and receive you to Myself, that where I am, there you may be also (John 14:1-3).

Peace I leave with you; My peace I give to you; not as the world gives do I give to you. Do not let your heart be troubled, nor let it be fearful (verse 27).

Dealing with Forgiving

Write down the names of those you need to forgive for an offense done to you. As you write each name, say aloud what he or she did and how it hurt you.

By faith, go back over the list and release to your Father in heaven each person and what he or she did. Ask the one true Judge to make all things right. In your heart, cut the chains holding the "rotting corpse of offense" off your back. Let God wash you clean and then leave the heavy burden of unforgiveness where it fell. Remind yourself of the wisdom in Colossians 3:13:

> Make allowance for each other's faults, and forgive anyone who offends you. Remember, the Lord forgave you, so you must forgive others (NLT).

Dealing with Other Issues

Before moving on, if there are any other weights and sins you are carrying, follow the same procedure. Write them down. Pray about them. Release them to God. Praise Him for giving you freedom through His Son, Jesus Christ.

The Final Act

For the final step in this exercise, fire up the paper shredder. What you are about to do is a picture of what has already taken place in your heart as you followed the wisdom of James 4:7-8:

Submit therefore to God.
Resist the devil and he will flee from you.
Draw near to God and He will draw near to you.
Cleanse your hands, you sinners;
and purify your hearts, you double-minded.

Rejoice as you take all the paper you've written on for this exercise and put it through the slot. Listen as the shredder does its work, rejoicing that God has already shredded and tossed everything you've confessed before Him. Listen as your guilt, shame, fear, and unforgiveness are shredded into little tiny pieces, never to be read again, never to be used again as an effective weapon against you.

Thanks be to God that His cleansing is thorough and final. He has chosen to take your sins far away from you and to remember them no more. Solidify this truth in your heart by meditating on the beautiful promises in Psalm 103:10-14:

> [God] has not dealt with us according to our sins, nor rewarded us according to our iniquities. For as high as the heavens are above the earth, so great is His lovingkindness toward those who fear Him. As far as the east is from the west, so far has He removed our transgressions from us. Just as a father has compassion on his children, so the LORD has compassion on those who fear Him. For He Himself knows our frame; He is mindful that we are but dust.

My prayer is that the truths from God's Word and the wisdom and life lessons He's given me have helped you—and will continue to help you—better navigate the sometimes treacherous roads of life. By following the steps presented in James 4:7-8 you are honoring God and you know He will never leave you stranded.

Until we meet at God's gracious feet and testify together regarding His marvelous ability to guide us safely home to heaven, I offer this lyric Steve wrote that I hope will become your heart's determination as firmly as it is mine.

Finish Well

I want to finish well.
I want to end this race
Still leaning on His amazing grace.
I want my last few miles to testify that God never fails.
I don't want to fall down this close to the line.
I want to finish well![1]

Now to Him who is able to keep you from stumbling, and to make you stand in the presence of His glory blameless with great joy, to the only God our Savior, through Jesus Christ our Lord, be glory, majesty, dominion and authority, before all time and now and forever. Amen (Jude 24).

Notes

Chapter 1: Trusting God's GPS
1. http://www.emailtidbits.com/Library/two_wolves_fighting.htm.
2. Annie Chapman, *Letting Go of Anger* (Eugene, OR: Harvest House Publishers, 2010), also published as *A Woman's Answer to Anger* (2002).

Chapter 5: Understanding What "Forgiven" Means
1. Spiro Zodiates, ThD, *The Hebrew-Greek Study Bible* (NASB) (Chattanooga, TN: AMG Publishers, 1977), s.v. *anamartétos.*

Chapter 6: Choosing Whose Voice You'll Listen To
1. Edward K. Rowell, ed., *Fresh Illustrations for Preaching and Teaching from Leadership Journal* (Grand Rapids, MI; Baker Books, 1997), p. 8.
2. Steve Chapman, "Unspoken Request," copyright © 2008 by Steve Chapman, Times and Seasons Music, BMI.

Chapter 7: Evicting Fear, Doubt, and Despair
1. Sherman L. Buford, "Fresh Illustrations for Preaching and Teaching," *Daily Devotional—Americas,* May 27, 2009, Family-Times.net.

Chapter 8: Refusing to Feel Discouraged
1. Sam George, Sermon Central, "Lou Nicholes," *lou@family-times.net,* January 15, 2010.
2. Steve Chapman, "Sweet on the Tongue," copyright © 2008 by Steve Chapman, Times and Seasons Music, BMI.

Chapter 10: Countering Self-pity Through Praise
1. Charles Swindoll, *The Greatest Life of All: Jesus* (Nashville: Thomas Nelson, 2008), p. 183.

Chapter 11: Kissing the Chains

1. John MacArthur, "Philippians," *The MacArthur New Testament Commentary* (Chicago: Moody Press, 2001), pp. 60-61.

2. "A Continuation of Mr. Bunyon's Life," www.chapellibrary.org/johnbunyon/volume-1.php, October 12, 2010.

3. Joni Eareckson Tada, "A Special Message from Joni," June 23, 2010, www.joniandfriends.org/blog/category/jonis-posts/?page=6.

4. Warren W. Wiersbe, *Be Joyful, A New Testament Study—Philippians* (Colorado Springs: Cook Communications Ministries, 2005), p. 17.

Chapter 12: Living Vibrantly, Chains and All

1. Steve Chapman, "The Man in Aisle Two," © 1995 by Steve Chapman, Times & Seasons Music, BMI, administered by Gaither Copyright Management.

2. Steve Chapman, "Love Her Back Home," copyright © 2006 by Steve Chapman, Times & Seasons Music, BMI.

Chapter 14: Living in Freedom

1. John MacArthur, "Matthew," *The MacArthur New Testament Commentary* (Chicago: Moody Press, 1985), p. 391.

Chapter 15: Setting Healthy Boundaries

1. John MacArthur, *Romans 1-8* (Chicago: Moody Press, 1991), p. 392.

2. Jerry Sittser, *A Grace Disguised* (Grand Rapids, MI: Zondervan, 2004), p. 41.

Chapter 17: Leaning on God's Grace

1. Steve Chapman, "Finish Well," © 2008 by Steve Chapman, Times & Seasons Music, BMI.

THE MOTHER-IN-LAW DANCE
Annie Chapman

When Two Women Love the Same Man...

Do you want to improve your relationship with your mother-in-law?
Could your relationship with your daughter-in-law be better?

Describing the often delicate relationship between mother-in-law and daughter-in-law as a dance, Annie Chapman candidly discusses the twists and turns of this connection and provides practical advice to help you better relate with your mother- or daughter-in-law. Drawing on years of experience, real-life input from other women, and biblical insights, Annie reveals simple steps to successfully—

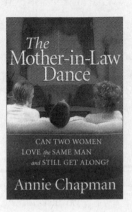

- build a great relationship
- deal with new traditions and activities
- overcome hurts and conflicts
- set realistic boundaries
- handle generation-gap issues
- accept (and reject) advice
- cope with differences in faith

As you establish a rhythm of love and grace, you'll find that you and your in-law can become friends—even close friends. *The Mother-in-Law Dance* will help you make that journey.

Hot Topics for Couples

Steve and Annie Chapman

. . . .

**Whether you are newlyweds or seasoned partners,
Hot Topics for Couples can help.**

What are the hot-button issues every couple struggles with? Drawing on 35-plus years of marriage, biblical wisdom, and survey responses, Steve and Annie reveal the difficult areas and offer practical ways to navigate them. You'll discover straightforward advice and conversation starters on topics that include...

- gender differences in sexuality
- "honey dos" and "honey don'ts" for both spouses
- leading, following, and making it work
- money, money, money
- the ups and downs of change

As an added bonus, interactive questions will help you and your mate develop an even stronger relationship. You can build a dynamic marriage based on love, cooperation, and flexibility that will become more joyful and satisfying every year!